*Making My Way in Ethics,
Worship, and Wood*

Making My Way in Ethics, Worship, and Wood

An Expository Memoir

William Johnson Everett

RESOURCE *Publications* · Eugene, Oregon

MAKING MY WAY IN ETHICS, WORSHIP, AND WOOD
An Expository Memoir

Copyright © 2021 William Johnson Everett. All rights reserved. Except for brief quotations in critical publications or reviews, no part of this book may be reproduced in any manner without prior written permission from the publisher. Write: Permissions, Wipf and Stock Publishers, 199 W. 8th Ave., Suite 3, Eugene, OR 97401.

Resource Publications
An Imprint of Wipf and Stock Publishers
199 W. 8th Ave., Suite 3
Eugene, OR 97401

www.wipfandstock.com

PAPERBACK ISBN: 978-1-6667-1914-7
HARDCOVER ISBN: 978-1-6667-1915-4
EBOOK ISBN: 978-1-6667-1916-1

OCTOBER 18, 2021

Contents

Introduction | ix

I. Foundations
Formation on the Potomac | 1
Emergence of the Basic Themes | 7
    Church and Public | 7
    Images, Symbols, and Ethics | 7
    Body, Person, and Society | 10
    Corporation, Covenant, and Association | 12
    Worship, Culture, and Ethics | 13

II. Frameworks
Disciplines in Transformation: Mapping the Connections of Christianity, Society, and Personality | 16
    The Disciplines: Christianity, Personality, and Society | 17
    The Dimensions: Loyalty, Theory, and Practice | 18
    The Approaches: Cultic, Prophetic, and Ecstatic | 18
    Connecting the Disciplines: The Triads | 20
        The Cultic Primary Triad | 21
        The Prophetic Primary Triad | 22
        The Ecstatic Primary Triad | 23
        The Secondary Triads | 23

Congruence | 25

    Simple Congruence | 26

    Functional Congruence | 26

    The Critical Task of Interdisciplinary Transformation | 28

    The Cabinet and the Contents | 29

III COMMITMENTS AND CONVICTIONS

  Land Ethics | 32

    Stewardship Ethics | 37

  The Hinge of Personal Transformation | 39

  God's Federal Republic | 40

    The Governing Symbol | 43

    Kingdom and Kingship | 44

    The Republican Vision | 46

    Federalism and Covenant | 48

      A Theory of Covenantal Publicity | 50

    A Psychological Theory: The Performer Self | 53

    Theological Transformations | 55

    A Retrospective Assessment | 58

  Blessed Be the Bond | 59

    The Subjects of Marriage | 61

    The Theological Symbols | 62

    Models of Relationship | 64

    The Harvest, the Winnowing, and the Bread | 65

    Issues and Outcomes | 65

IV PRACTICES

  The OIKOS Project on Work, Family, and Faith | 68

  Ministerial Education and the Doctor of Ministry Program | 72

  Religion, Federalism, and the Struggle for Public Life | 73

The Churches and Germany's "Peaceful Revolution" | 76

Religious Organizations and Constitutional Justice in India | 80

Sacred Lands and Religious Assemblies in America | 85

The Pacific Homes Case | 88

Native American Sacred Lands | 90

Assessment, Evaluation, and Consolidation | 94

Covenantal Publicity and Reconciliation | 98

South Africa: Reconciliation and a New Constitution | 99

Reconciliation and the Vietnam War Memorial | 101

Reconciliation as a Journey | 102

Journey and Place | 103

Praying for God's Republic | 104

The Dialogue of Ethics and Worship | 105

The Purposes of Worship | 105

Political Theory as the Partner of a Theology of Worship | 107

The Principles for Regeneration of Worship | 108

Practical and Critical Ethical Considerations | 111

V Beyond Prose

Wood and Word | 113

The Roundtable Project: Worship and the Work of Reconciliation | 114

Roundtable Worship and Peace-Building | 119

Red Clay, Blood River: Reconciliation, Ecology, and Narrative | 120

Turning from Prose to Poetry and Song | 126

Sawdust and Soul | 129

Mining Memories and the Work of Reconciliation | 131

Recollection | 136

Bibliography | 139

Introduction

In this book I set down in concise manner the main concepts, theories, and commitments that have arisen in the context of my life story. I have called this record an expository memoir, because it seeks to lift up these concepts in the context of my remembered life and give them some orderly presentation. It exposes not only the contours of my intellectual life but the cultural context that shaped them. In that sense it is like the traditional expository sermon that seeks to lift out the meaning of the writings that have arisen in the history of ancient Israel and the early church. There are other ways we try to make sense of our life in this world, whether through visual arts, craftwork, music, or spiritual intuition. These ways of being, doing, and making surround and shape my conceptual thinking, but in this little book I mainly want to lift up the way my thinking has engaged the world as I came to know and act in it. Especially in my latter years, the crafting of wood, songs, poetry, and worship has emerged to give other forms to the vision expressed in my intellectual work, and so I will reflect on these efforts as well.

Our lives have many dimensions—physical, geographic, emotional, historical, spiritual, relational, and intellectual. No thought occurs apart from a body living in a specific environment and time. This does not mean we reduce all our ways of thinking and acting to our biological or cultural identities. It simply affirms that we all occupy different moments and places on the world's stages, engaged in constantly changing arguments and dramas as we seek to share the same world. While it is impossible to trace out all the ways these various dimensions interact, whether in our thoughts or our emotions or relationships, I want to recall key elements of my personal history in order to understand my intellectual journey and communicate its meaning to others. The journey will take us from the unique world of

Introduction

Washington, DC, to a historically Black college in Arkansas, Berlin's Wall between East and West, South Africa's Robben Island, India's construction of a Constitution, and the longing for the integrity and peace of Cyprus—and many other places in between.

My account lays out the way I turned to ethics in my early years and to the exploration of the connection of the social and psychological sciences to Christian ethics. Fundamental concepts of covenant, ecclesiology, public life, and the "oikos" of work, family, and faith then began to emerge to guide my later substantive commitments. These in turn found practical ramifications in worship, theological education, restorative justice, land use, and family life. In my latter years I found new avenues of expression guided by these underlying concerns in poetry, song, liturgy, and woodcraft.

As I proceed I will describe the experiences that have guided and shaped the way of thinking emerging in that context. These thoughts have not simply been bubbles emerging from a turtle's underwater swim, but are threads with ongoing histories, gaining a woven form at a particular time but continuing into subsequent thoughts. Just as my mind always sought out connections among very disparate realities, so this little book seeks to connect these thoughts as they unfolded in my life. Thus, this memoir is conceived not only as a journey but also as a kind of ongoing tapestry woven from many connected threads. Whether or not this mirrors your own tapestry, I hope it can be a conversation partner for your own effort to understand your life and its possible covenants and callings.

I

Foundations

Formation on the Potomac

When people hear that I grew up in Washington, DC, they sometimes exclaim "So that explains it!" Well, as they say, it's more complicated than that. How, indeed, did I begin with a youth immersed in a world of government and national monuments and end by writing poetry and liturgies and building furniture, especially round communion tables? Like many others, I come to my late years asking what threads of thought and commitment have held my life together on this winding way.

Born in Washington in 1940, I grew up along the Potomac River. Only now, in writing this, am I aware that the name Potomac is an ancient Algonquian word with a contested meaning. How fitting that this river situates me not only within Native American memory but also on the dividing line between North and South in our Civil War. Along that river my Massachusetts great-grandfather was wounded at the Battle of Antietam and subsequently decided to move his young family to Washington after the war. I carried the sermons of Puritan and Independent ancestors in my ears, the fractured history of my American forebears—some Tories, some Revolutionaries—in my bones. My birth name, William Wade Everett, III, signaled this sense of family legacy and remained until my second marriage, in 1982, when I took on my wife's family name as a sign of a new beginning in my life.

Making My Way in Ethics, Worship, and Wood

When I was two, my mother took me and my two sisters to Mamaroneck, New York, to be near her parents while my father served in the Navy for three years in Pearl Harbor. The rest of my childhood revolved around the cultural monuments, churches, businesses, and governmental panoply of Washington and around a dairy farm an hour away in Virginia started by my grandfather and his cousin, a veterinarian. From my great uncle's perspective, it was to be a way to explore new methods of breeding and farming. From my grandfather's perspective, it was probably a way to have a summer retreat and be a gentleman farmer. They called it Overbrook Farms. My father inherited it after his father's death in 1949.

I spent all my summers there playing in the gardens, woods, and fields, fishing in the farm's lake, swimming and playing golf at the local 9-hole country club, where errant balls often took me over the barbed wire into a cow pasture. When I was older I began to work in the fields harvesting grains and corn with men from the six families on the farm. They included old mountain folks as well as Harold Fairfax, a quiet John Henry type of man, who, I felt at the time, must have lived there since slavery. He taught me how to shock wheat. He could lift a ten-gallon container of milk with each arm and place it on the delivery truck. I lived in a world where black and white were close but not equal. While I tried to act personally as if it were not so, the way to a broader transformation was beyond my young horizon. In the fields I helped stack hay bales on the wagons. In the late summer I was sent up in the silo (being the littlest) and spread the chopped corn coming down from the pipe to keep the leaves from spreading to the edges. No mask was provided, to say the least.

There was the Fewell family, old mountain folk, loyal to the core, who suffered and loved the land even as they couldn't escape it. I went fishing with Charlie Fewell, whose mind was crushed from early on, and whose gentle spirit was blown out by a passing car on the highway as he rode his bike to town. The driver must not have been local, because everyone knew about Charlie and his meandering ways on the highway. It was the first funeral I can remember. His Uncle Earl and his father before him took care of my grandparents' house, yard, and garden as if it were their own.

There were other farm families too, the Cores and Simpsons and the Garrisons as well as Effie Reed, a diminutive and wiry Black woman whose connection to us and to the land was strong although opaque and immemorial to my early eyes. My college roommate and life-long friend Eric

Greenleaf, born and raised in Brooklyn, New York, claimed that I had lived on a plantation. Maybe he was right.

The image of that farm still informs my thought and imagination. I learned to work with tools large and small. I came to understand that a farm is a repair waiting to happen. My father hated a derelict barn. Today Loudoun County is the richest county per capita in the nation, littered with trophy homes where 80 dairy farms once prospered. I feel like Rip van Winkel when I return for visits. Nichols Hardware, in the nearby town of Purcellville, still keeps the fishing gear in the same corner as it did 60 years ago, but Madeline Albright and Ollie North are its customers. The mayor as I write is an African American.

My life in Washington accustomed me to meeting people from all over the world, to thinking of government as something familiar and personal, to participating in a church life aware of global pluralism. Even our venerable downtown Calvary Baptist Church, currently pastored by a lesbian couple, was dually aligned with American (Northern) and Southern Baptist Conventions. I was the fourth generation to worship there. We regularly passed Washington's first mosque on our way to church, built when I was in my early teens. The same Sunday commute took us past the White House, the Treasury department, and Pennsylvania Avenue. It also took us past the shaded Sunday windows of Woodward and Lothrop, the beloved Washington department store where three generations of my family had worked, along with various cousins and friends. My father subtly warned me away. I think he knew my mind and spirit would never fit there. He was right.

I can see now how growing up in this milieu disposed me to the task of connecting things in otherwise separate compartments—religion, politics, farming, the land, race, and nationality. "Connections" became a theme in my life. I even remember, when I was only four, tying together all the furniture in the living room so that you couldn't move one piece without moving the others. To say the least, this expression of an enduring value did not please my mother.

As I moved into my school years, this search for connecting things led me to try to figure out the whole context in which to connect them. In eighth grade I wrote a paper on "The History of Life" for my beloved science teacher, William Harrison. With that topic nailed down, I was ready to proceed! I signed all my science papers with a small drawing of a centipede, taking the name "Myriapoda" as my nickname. I don't know why. Maybe it was the idea of coordinating all those feet.

Along with this penchant for connecting disparate things, I also spent many hours in the summer constructing an elaborate village in the dirt under our cottage at the farm. I called it Smallville and set up its own rules and institutions. The roads, I recall, were always a problem. Like many children, I could retreat into this utopian world far from the parental realities on the floor above. To my amazement, my own daughters also engaged in such an elaborate utopian fantasy of their own design as they were growing up. I even invited them to present their village to my Church and Society class as an example of our deep longing for a perfect society. Perhaps this inclination to utopian construction also figured in my later decision to pursue a career in social ethics.

In my final three years of high school I attended St. Albans School at the Washington National Cathedral. At its center stood, two-thirds complete, a Gothic Cathedral that sought in Anglican style to bring together Christian faith and the spiritual life of the nation. Exposure to the sonorities of chant and organ in that still uncompleted vault have never left me, even as I have reacted against the patriarchy and monarchy of the words and sentiments behind them. Because of its spiritual mission to the nation, the Cathedral opened its arms to the diversity of Washington's people, indigenous and foreign. Indeed, my student friends included Muslims from Iraq and Pakistan, a prominent rabbi's son, several Catholics, and a range of Protestants, including myself, the Baptist. The extraordinary man who taught me German was a refugee Russian artist named George Gabritchewsky, who had painted for the Romanovs and their aristocracy. Despite this heterogeneity, it was only after I left in 1958 that the school graduated its first African-American in 1964. In 2017 the Cathedral removed a stained glass window honoring Confederate Generals Robert E. Lee and Thomas "Stonewall" Jackson.

As in this public life, so my comfortable home life had deep-seated internal fractures as well. My parents had a number of physical and psychological difficulties in their lives and relationship, so that our relative wealth always had a strange emptiness or incompleteness to it. My father struggled in a business life he never really chose and which he only loved for the people in it. He had gone to MIT to become a chemical engineer but the Great Depression undercut his plans and he returned to the security of the store where he was a third-generation employee. His deep frustrations in life led to severe depression when I was in my early teens (when I too was consumed by a passion for chemistry).

FOUNDATIONS

From my father I received a deep, indeed stringent conscience and a sense of practical ethical commitment. From my mother I received a passionate spirituality and aesthetic sensibility that lay largely buried until mid-life. It was my father's struggle for a life of faithful economic and community stewardship that dominated my primary career. It is my mother's aesthetic and spiritual search, though not her language and theology, that I have come to integrate into my life more adequately in these later years.

Within this diversity and these vaguely conscious disjunctions I often played and worked alone. While sociable and friendly, I enjoyed the solitudes of fishing, taking things apart and putting things together, hiking, reading, and writing. In my teenage years I was fascinated by the caves along the Shenandoah Valley and beneath the limestone ridges beyond in West Virginia. I was always to some degree on the periphery of things as I tried to bring the different circles of my life together without being fully anchored in any one. I tried to be a diplomat in a city of diplomats and negotiators. In my family, I tried to be the mediator from my position as the middle child between two sisters. Sometimes, though, I could be moved to direct action, as when I formed a "Nature Club" at the age of twelve and tore up the surveyors' stakes in our nearby woods to prevent the destruction of the trees. I think the statute of limitations has closed out prosecution on that point, but Washington sprawled in spite of my resistance until it engulfed the family's farm when I was in my forties, yet another psychic blow in my father's life of depression and courageous good cheer.

The impulses I received from my mother emerged transformed later in life, but were not totally buried in my early years. For several Christmases, starting about the age of ten, I put together a little home service with my sisters, both of whom took up piano, while I was leader of the liturgy (though I didn't know that term then). In spite of our upbringing in fairly plain Protestant practices, it became a core experience for me of ritual, symbol, and liturgy. In subsequent years the liturgy, music, and architecture of my St. Albans experience seeded life-long interests in worship and its connection to public life. My English teachers there planted seeds of appreciation for poetry and public speech that survived within the borders of my academic career and social activism. In my senior year I became the leader of the Conservative position in the school's Government Class, at one point even having the privilege of "debating" Dean Acheson, the former Secretary of State, who was a friend of the school.

As I look back now I can see more clearly the meaning of my senior paper at St. Albans, where I also was the editorial editor of the school newspaper. It was a historical study of *The Daily Worker*, the official newspaper of the Communist Party of the USA. In those days a mere high school student could walk into the Library of Congress and make use of its vast resources! In addition, I could sit for some hours in the library of the American Legion, which, in its anti-Communist zeal (it was the height of the McCarthy Red Scare), had a complete file of the paper. What underlay this choice of topic? I think it was the conjunction of concern for the nation's spiritual integrity and an awareness of the room for a radical critique of the injustice I was beginning to sense around me. My well-researched paper was written from within the viewpoint of a conservative Washington establishment that was confident it had assuaged the worst of American labor's complaints, leaving *The Daily Worker* as a pitiful mouthpiece of Soviet propaganda. Issues of race, not to speak of gender, were still on the margins of my awareness if not my experience. This conflict of establishment upbringing and emerging awareness of the suffering and injustice around me developed into a dominant pattern in my life's tapestry.

These are some of the formative experiences that became the emotional foundation of the intellectual journey that began to unfold in my late adolescence. While my mother and some others thought that I would be a minister, I never could envision the role as something that could hold my intellectual life or my buried passions, and so I aimed for university and the teaching life, albeit with religious themes to guide it.

Emergence of the Basic Themes

With this base of experience and education I began to lay out four basic themes in my years of study at Wesleyan University, Yale Divinity School, and Harvard University. While I developed a keen interest in music at Wesleyan under Richard Winslow, my chorus director and teacher, at one time having some formal conversations with the composer John Cage, these themes were all directing me to what became a career in ethics within a broadly Christian perspective.

FOUNDATIONS

Church and Public

My chief mentor at Wesleyan, Kenneth Underwood, led me into an abiding interest in the relation of the church to public life. When the political philosopher Hannah Arendt came to Wesleyan for a semester, she left in my conversation concepts of public life that deeply shape me to this day. In my second year I joined the newly formed College of Social Studies, a curricular and pedagogical experiment that sought to integrate history, economics, government, philosophy, and ethics within a system of tutorials, seminars, and weekly papers. With Underwood's guidance I began to be aware of the structural and organizational differences between Protestant and Catholic churches and how church orders and practices shape ethical life at the personal and institutional level. His Yale colleague James Gustafson came to the College of Social Studies to examine me in my junior year and then accompanied me as mentor and friend until his recent death at the age of 95. His own work, beginning with *Treasure in Earthen Vessels*, introduced me to the theological and sociological significance of ecclesiology in the relation between Christian ethics and public policy.

Images, Symbols, and Ethics

To examine these relationships in specific detail I drew on the idea that our ethical action is shaped by the deep images we bring to our work, images that are also presented in symbols and liturgies of worship. Images of prophets, teachers, and healers shape how we exercise our roles in life. Images of "Kingdom of God," and of table fellowship, for instance, shape our purposes in action and our search for the good life. This method informed my honors thesis on the leaders of programs of social action and evangelism in the American Baptist Convention (now called the American Baptist Churches USA). It would continue throughout my future research and writing as it was refined to focus on symbolism and ritual practice. Drawing on Paul Tillich's notion of the "theonomous" Protestant approach to religion and culture, I became committed to a path between the imposition of a social blueprint or moral code "from above" and an individualistic piety "from below" to embrace a "liturgical drama that unlocks the everyday to reveal the eternal."[1] In this drama the wrestling of each individual within the fabric of social responsibility, duties, and powers became a

---

1. Everett, "Baptists and Politics," 110.

concluding note to my thesis as well as a constant basso continuo in my own succeeding life.

In looking through this thesis I am struck by my complete innocence about matters of gender. "Men" occupy the only field of reference for public actors, for instance. Stylistically, I can see my use of poetic imagery adorning numerous sentences. What was a stylistic matter here became a full-blown commitment to poetry itself only in my retirement. Most importantly, my focus on the intersection of theology, ecclesiology, symbolism, and American public life was already clearly foundational to my intellectual life. The task of reconstructing Christian theology in a way that could more effectively engage that public life was a beckoning light. An interest in the relation of aesthetics to ethics, nurtured by my Wesleyan experience as well as my reading of Alfred North Whitehead's philosophy, emerged clearly toward the end of this work and was reflected in the address I gave as the student speaker at my Wesleyan Commencement in 1962. In the heady language of that brief oration, I declaimed that "To combine the quality of dance with the style of service may be a proper synthesis of the liberal arts tradition with the new world stage."

When I got to Yale Divinity School that fall, the Civil Rights struggle was entering its trial by fire. I had already met Martin Luther King Jr. at Wesleyan and was amazed and inspired by his sense of inner peace and outer non-violence. Even as marches, sit-ins, and demonstrations were pulsing in the life around me, I was also struggling with the emotional task of coming to maturity. And for this, the meaning of symbols elaborated by Freud and Jung served not only my interest in religious symbols but also my inner struggle for emotional development and sexual intimacy. It was at this time that I learned to play the folk guitar and began to absorb an extensive repertoire of songs from the movements around me and from my Appalachian past. The absorption in song was a way to tie together the love of singing I had cultivated at Wesleyan and my sense of the lyrical word with my emerging social consciousness.

In my first seminary summer I went to Germany to spend three months with Gerd Decke, a Fulbright exchange student at Wesleyan, who has been a constant friend to this day. An account of our numerous adventures over the years would fill a small book of its own. I went to Berlin's Free University with him a few months after The Wall had gone up and heard John Kennedy speak to the student body in June of 1963, even as we spent many evenings going over to East Berlin for conversations with students there. The struggle with the meaning of Marxist critique and Communist practice that began with my study of *The Daily Worker* was given new intensity, a focus that continued in my research, teaching, and writing until the collapse of Soviet Communism and its Eastern European satellites twenty-five years later.

In my second seminary summer I served as a substitute teacher at Philander Smith College in Little Rock, Arkansas, a Black Methodist college that was a beneficiary of a Carnegie grant to free up faculty for further training. The Freedom Rides had taken place a year earlier. Civil rights workers James Chaney, Michael Schwerner, and Andrew Goodman were murdered across the Mississippi River two weeks after I arrived. In spite of these horrific events, I devoted my energy to my students, who taught me how far removed my academic training was from their lives and needs. I only hope I didn't do much harm. It was a very hard summer. I emerged even more aware of how deeply symbols and rituals, from those of the Ku Klux Klan to the songs of the civil rights movement, shape our ethical action and link thought to practice. It was also a time of becoming aware once again of the brutal injustice just beneath the surface of our society, not far removed from the German experience of the Nazis and the Holocaust.

In the midst of this political turmoil, and only partially resolving issues of sexual and emotional maturity, I made the decision to marry a fellow student and set out on the task of building a family. The marriage was not built on the love it needed to survive, but it produced three talented, caring, and intelligent children with whom I learned the depth of parental love and the resilience of filial attachment. The failure of this marriage after fifteen years and my subsequent marriage to my beloved Sylvia deeply shaped my later thought in obvious as well as subtle and indirect ways.

These searing emotional experiences led me to see more deeply the way symbols are always embodied images. We experience them viscerally as well as intellectually. In my graduate work at Harvard, beginning in 1965, I returned to the writings of Norman O. Brown, who had been an influential teacher at Wesleyan, as well as to broader cultural studies, and became fascinated with how we use the body as a metaphor with deep symbolic power to integrate our intellectual, social, and ethical life. At that point, I couldn't achieve this integration in my own bodily life, but I set about seeing what role this potent image had played in church and society and might play in the future.

Making My Way in Ethics, Worship, and Wood

Body, Person, and Society

At Harvard, my effort to understand the body symbol guided my work in various fields, including Eastern religion, political theory, biblical studies, ethics and ecclesiology, psychology, sociology, and art. The Second Vatican Council was in the middle of its work to bring the Roman Catholic Church's thought and practice into critical engagement with the modern world. One of the central struggles in that council was between those who saw the church as "The Body of Christ," a traditional formulation with hierarchical values, and those who used the biblical image of "People of God," with its more democratic and historical emphases.

At the same time, sparked by discovering the work of Shailer Mathews on the way theological symbols are embedded in social practices, I was entering more deeply into the connection between theology and social structure generally. This theological awareness was augmented by my immersion in the sociological perspectives on religion flowing from the work of Max Weber. Since then, I have always been strongly attuned to the sociological function of theological symbols, especially as I honed in on the function of patriarchal symbols in theology and social ideology.

Out of my research at Harvard emerged a doctoral dissertation on "Body Thinking" that explored how and why many cultures use the body metaphorically to evoke loyalty for social organizations. Indeed, body thinking orients many people to the world and their own life meaning in general. In this dissertation I first showed how the image of the Body of Christ had four meanings in Christian history and thought. The historical body was that of Jesus of Nazareth in Roman-occupied Galilee. The second body was his resurrected, or glorious, body. The third was the body known in the Eucharistic communion. It is the bread and wine that is his body and blood. The fourth body was the Church itself. Each use of the body symbol contains different meanings, whether of the body as the seat of ethical, historical action, of transcendence over death, of sacrifice, or of corporate unity. Because of the symbolic power of the body, loyalties attached to one of its meanings, such as the bread and wine of communion, become attached to other meanings, such as the institutional church. The multi-valence of the symbol as well as its connection to the indispensable physical basis of our individual lives give it immense psychological, cultural and social power.

Thus, the body symbol is a powerful way of identifying individual embodied selves with the wider loyalties of the church, the body politic, the body of human knowledge, and even the body of the cosmos. It functions to summon us to sacrifice our immediate physical bodies for the more enduring and expansive "body" that we also inhabit. It is a powerful way to justify and motivate the defense of our lives against outside enemies and to survive beyond their threats. Indeed, our modern notion of the corporation can be traced back to the idea of the Body of Christ (*corpus Christi*) which has conquered death. In its immortality our fleeting lives can find meaning and memorialization. As a body the corporation can claim legal rights as a person as well as own, sell, contract with, sue, and be sued by other corporate entities and individuals. In contemporary American Constitutional law it can even claim a civil right such as free speech. Thus, the impact of the Church's claim to be the Body of Christ continues in the corporate forms of American economic and political life.

As a model for our relationships, the body symbol has traditionally been tied to a model of the body in which the head rules the members, thus legitimating hierarchical patterns of organization. While its most obvious example is the military command of the captain (from *caput*, meaning head) over the troops (the *corps*), it also is extended to religious institutions, as when the Pope, as head of the church, is held to rightfully rule over the church's members.

The ethical question for the thesis was whether this deeply ingrained body symbol could serve democratic purposes or was inherently opposed to them. Using the theories of political scientist Karl Deutsch, who was also one of my advisors, I argued that contemporary theories of communication and control ("cybernetics") could provide a different model for interpreting the body, thus bringing together the symbols of "Body of Christ" and "People of God." Though I think Karl Deutsch had some inkling of this, I couldn't foresee at the time how the digital revolution would upend traditional politics in revolutionary ways that reveal in new ways our human bent toward fearful oppression as well as altruistic justice.

During my research for this thesis on body thinking I spent a summer investigating how the concept of "person" (*persona*) had developed out of the old Latin term for dramatic masks (and perhaps even older Etruscan ceremonies about entry into the underworld). To have a persona was to be equipped to join in the drama and play a role. It was the basis for having voice in the action. Persona came to be used in legal settings as the capacity to appear in the drama of the trial and then was taken over into theology by Tertullian and Augustine, where it was used in the Western church to speak of the three ways in which God is manifest as Father, Son, and Holy Spirit. In our own time it descended from this heavenly sphere to attach a divine creativity to every individual—man or woman, slave or free, black, white, red, or brown. Individual human beings received "personalities" through which they manifested the divine creativity and autonomy. We are still living out the implications of this concept's heritage in the democratization of family and society for the sake of personal freedom. It lies at the root of the deep conflict over the status of the human being developing in women's wombs.

Corporation, Covenant, and Association

The notion that a basic symbol like that of the body could take on various models of organization remained a key insight for later work. What I could not adequately articulate then was the alternative theory of social organization that could take us beyond the organic theories of society historically legitimated by the body symbol. Although my key teacher at Harvard, James Luther Adams, immersed me in theories of covenant and voluntary association, I did not develop these lines of thought more fully until later. I think this limitation was partly because I was still struggling to work through my own personal agenda with body images and their symbolic meanings. It was only later, with a more adequate resolution of these struggles within myself, that I came to explore the riches of covenant's impact on the development of Western ideas of federalism and its structuring of vital publics and republics.

As I look back, these ideas constitute the basic elements that I drew on through much of my career: the role of symbols and images in ethics, and the key concepts of public and ecclesia, body and person, covenant and federalism, and voluntary association. There was only one element, buried in my farm experience, that was waiting to flower later—the oikos and ecology.

Worship, Culture, and Ethics

With my work at Harvard completed, I was offered a position at St. Francis Seminary School of Pastoral Ministry in Milwaukee, Wisconsin. Under the impact of the reforms of the Second Vatican Council (1962-65), the faculty leaders there wanted to put together a program in theology and social science. Since my work on the body image in ecclesiology had devoted a good deal of research to the Council's work, I felt peculiarly suited to this task. They must have felt the same, since this venerable Roman Catholic institution let this wet-behind-the-ears Baptist ethicist into their midst as a colleague in this educational mission. In spite of the fact that the winters would be cold and the actual religious environment unknown, I began this work at St. Francis Seminary in the fall of 1969, taking my wife and son with me. It was a post I was to hold for fifteen years.

While the immediate task of working out a theory of interdisciplinary engagement occupied center stage, the Seminary's life of worship and formation began to deepen my appreciation of symbols, worship, and the ritual formation of personal and public life. My move to Milwaukee also opened me up to Catholic cultures I had not experienced before. I encountered a piety informed by descendants of German socialists, Slavic immigrants, and a medley of adventurous and often radical spirits that had flowered in adverse circumstances far from the usual centers of Catholic ecclesiastical dominion. All of this bubbled in the cauldron of social conflict and experimentation that coursed through American life in the early seventies.

One of my first writings in that period, presented at the annual meeting of the Society of Christian Ethics in 1972, was an article, "Liturgy and American Society: An Invocation to Ethical Analysis," about the way various institutional sectors of American life had their legitimating "cults," whether they be sports, entertainment, the university, or politics. By "cult" I simply meant any ritual symbolic activity that rehearsed people's central loyalties and perspectives on the world. These cults give us the language we can use to be persons in the public dramas around us. In that sense, "cult" is the heart of "culture," the basis for legitimating any social institution. In order to assess these institutions from an ethical standpoint we had to understand these cultic activities, whether they be a Pledge of Allegiance, a football spectacle, or an academic commencement. All of this bore directly on whether and how the churches could or should engage this panoply of cultic life. Behind this ethical analysis lay a concern first awakened in me by my Harvard teacher Robert Bellah, whose work on civil religion has continued to inform my thought over the years.

This concern for how institutions use cult to anchor themselves in culture was a move away from concentrating on power politics and immediate public policy. In the conceptual framework of Talcott Parsons, Bellah's senior colleague at Harvard, it was a movement from "society" and its institutions to "culture" and its symbols, rituals, and values. In a sense this focus went back to my life in Washington and the National Cathedral, where people tried to create a kind of religious culture to cultivate institutions to process, adjudicate, negotiate, and perhaps resolve the intense political pressures arising from a diverse and conflicted country. Much of the Washington I knew was devoted to creating the cultural glue that might hold together the fissiparous individuals, groups, and states as a United States of America. As if to mirror this cultural work of integration, my family still made ritual pilgrimages to the corn field at Antietam, Maryland, where my great-grandfather was wounded. Memorials to the Civil War that had nearly severed the Union littered the landscape of my youth. As a boy I read the ten volumes of *The Photographic History of the Civil War* from end to end more than once. As I was growing up, the country was still going through an intense struggle to redefine itself in the light of Lincoln's wartime vision. The formation of legitimate institutions to adjudicate conflict was not only historically real for me, it also fit my personal sensibilities as a peace-seeking diplomat.

In the mid nineteen-seventies, in the wake of the misuses of civil religion to justify our intervention in Vietnam and the positive uses of it in the civil rights movement, I wrote a little piece for a regional meeting of the American Academy of Religion in Chicago wondering about the "disestablishment" of this civil religion, not only for Constitutional reasons but also to expose the peril of idolatry for the churches' too-easy incorporation of symbols like the American flag into their sanctuaries and worship life. Here again, as in much other work, I sought to trace a path of critical engagement between church and public life rather than simple accommodation or estrangement. This was deepened by my appropriation of the perspectives of H. R. Niebuhr, whose teaching flowed to me through Kenneth Underwood and James Gustafson. Unfortunately, Niebuhr died the summer before I reached Yale, and so I was unable to work with him directly.

This interest in the legitimating role of symbols also led me to engage more deeply with political theory and ecclesiology. While my doctoral thesis had arisen in a dialogue between Catholic ecclesiology and the cybernetic political theory of Karl Deutsch, I also was continuing to engage the thought of Hannah Arendt. In 1972 I prepared a paper on ecclesiology and political theory within a framework of some of her crucial concepts. Arendt's fertile reflections on the meaning of the public, private, and social realms informed my understanding of the church as a public, taking seriously the original meaning of the Greek word *ekklesia* as a public assembly. This idea would continue to resonate in my thought to the present day. Whereas many people, including Arendt, continued to see the church as a private gathering of family-like relationships, I would always argue that its existence as a genuine, though unusual, public would define the proper core of the church's life and mission.

I presented this paper, "Ecclesiology and Political Authority," at the 1973 annual meeting of the Society of Christian Ethics. I had the remarkable privilege of meeting her there and hearing her comments on my paper. Ecclesiology, of course, was far from her usual field of concerns, so it was hard for her to comment on it in any depth, but I was deeply grateful to have touched the orbit of someone who in my opinion was one of the foremost intellectual figures of the twentieth century.

II

Frameworks

Disciplines in Transformation: Mapping the Connections of Christianity, Society, and Personality

OVER THE YEARS I had become committed to a critical engagement among the fields of theology, the social sciences, and psychology. At some level, I had always wondered about the seemingly automatic connections my parents, especially my mother, had made between their Christian faith and public policy or views of personal psychology. As my circle of conversation had expanded, I had become more aware of how Christian views could differ radically from each other and have quite different entanglements with views of society and personality. As I entered my teaching career, the connecting ropes of my boyhood became an elaborate effort to trace the links between religious faith and social and psychological approaches to life.

In my second year at St. Francis I was joined by Tim (T. J.) Bachmeyer, a University of Chicago graduate in the field of theology and psychology. We started to teach these subjects in a common course on theology and the behavioral sciences. In the summer of 1973 we spent over a month at the Institute for Ecumenical and Cultural Research on the campus of St. John's University and Abbey at Collegeville, Minnesota, to lay out the basic contours of a book to serve as a framework for this interdisciplinary work. Our growing families accompanied us and enjoyed the quiet beauty of the woods, meadows, and lake around us. The campus's institutions have remained an important reference point for me, especially as they set about producing the glorious St. John's Bible, the first illuminated hand-written Bible since the Middle Ages. Copies of the Heritage edition of this Bible formed the centerpiece to a conference on "The Arts of Peace" that my wife Sylvia and I chaired at Lake Junaluska, North Carolina, in 2019.

Over the next five years the syllabus of this course fed into a book that set forth our framework for this critical engagement. It appeared in 1979 as *Disciplines in Transformation: A Guide to Theology and the Behavioral Sciences*. After Tim left the school and entered private practice, I continued to teach the course with other colleagues, especially Rev. Kenneth Metz and Rev. Arthur Heinz, whose work in pastoral care continued to anchor the course in pastoral practice. The book was picked up by some others teaching in this area, including my good friend Glen Stassen at Southern Baptist Theological Seminary in Louisville, Kentucky.

Gregory Baum, a well-known Catholic scholar and activist in Toronto, wrote an extensive summary and critique of *Disciplines*, which he put in his journal *The Ecumenist* in July-August 1981. I had met Baum in the course of my work at St. Francis and still am struck by the depth at which he grasped this work and his passionately prophetic critique of it. Drawing on his outline, here is a brief description of the framework of the book.

The Disciplines: Christianity, Personality, and Society

The first step in building this framework was to describe the three partners in this engagement—Christianity, Personality, and Society. We came to call these "disciplines," since we were trying to understand them as fields of knowledge as well as of practice and an underlying set of primary values. The theoreticians committed to these three partners are generally called theologians, psychologists, and sociologists, respectively. Their compatriots in practice include pastors and Christian educators, psychiatrists and counselors, and social planners, politicians, and community organizers. Our work among people preparing for a professional life in ministry helped us to pay close attention to these three dimensions, a perspective that a strictly academic position might have foreshortened.

The Dimensions: Loyalty, Theory, and Practice

Each of these disciplines is constituted by theories, practices, and loyalties. These are the "dimensions" of a discipline. A loyalty is the highest orienting and motivating core of a discipline. Christianity has loyalties like Kingdom of God, Body of Christ, Church, Jesus, the Bible, the cross, the resurrection, and other key doctrines and images. We usually call this cluster of loyalties their "faith," but the other disciplines also have their faiths as well. Disciplines devoted to personality seek health, fulfillment, optimal functioning, "ego over id," and "capacity for love and work." Disciplines focused on society may seek justice, harmony, equality, societal survival, or rule of law. All of them entertain notions of truth underlying their epistemologies.

Each of them generates various theories that seek to comprehend this truth in a coherent, arguable, and transmittable way. Just as Christianity has many theological traditions, so too do the disciplines focused on personality and society. Theories provide the ways we describe the subject matter of these disciplines, even though the efficacy of such a descriptive vocabulary is always limited. Theories are always tested by experience, by evidence of their incompleteness, or manifestations of their illogicality.

Finally, we find a welter of alternative practices in each. Christianity includes practices of prayer, worship, personal piety, social advocacy and welfare, as well as forms of organization and preferred societal engagement. Psychologists can take many therapeutic and clinical paths to implement their theories and loyalties. Within society we see many political parties, programs, and means of social construction and reconstruction.

The Approaches: Cultic, Prophetic, and Ecstatic

Within each of these disciplines people have brought together theories, practices and loyalties to create some perennial "approaches" that orient and shape their thought and action. In describing these approaches within the three disciplines, we drew on the "ideal type" analysis of Max Weber, a towering presence in the sociology of my early years. An ideal type is a configuration of characteristics that illuminates the main themes within a field of inquiry, whether religion, society, or personality, in a somewhat coherent way. They help us ask critical questions about the power and weakness of a particular way of living or thinking.

FRAMEWORKS

In Christianity we identified three approaches: Cultic, Prophetic, and Ecstatic. In this we were re-working the categories used by Ernst Troeltsch in *The Social Teaching of the Christian Churches*. Cultic approaches focus on the life of worship, symbol, ritual, and story. Practices of priesthood, devotion, prayer, sacrament, and ritual occupy the heart of the Christian life. Prophetic Christians are centered in the biblical ethical precepts, the work of judgment and ethical struggle, and the ethical teachings of Jesus, including his invocation of the Kingdom of God that is coming to transform the world. Ecstatic Christians focus on the inner life of the Spirit that takes us out of our normal ways. Ecstasy literally means "standing outside ourselves." It may be very mystical, leading to monastic silence, or it may be very expressive, emotional, and lively, as in Pentecostal practices. The key loyalty is the emphasis on inner personal experience of the Holy Spirit as the way God is present in the world.

This framework of approaches was not meant to fit everything into neat boxes. Being ideal types, approaches end up blending elements of each other, with any approach placing one of the three ideal configurations at the center and adding the others in a subordinate manner. However, we felt that these three types exert a strong attraction on people within Christianity. They are three basic ways Christians have brought together their loyalties, theories, and practices.

We then examined how the three dimensions have been organized in the behavioral sciences as well. Society can be approached as a Systemic, a Dualistic, or a Pluralistic reality. Systemic approaches are typified by organic theories of society that see it as some kind of body or very complex machine. Societies exist and survive because they fulfill basic functions, as Talcott Parsons pointed out in the nineteen-fifties and sixties. If they do not, they decline and die. Discerning these functions and the organs or structures that serve them is the task of theoreticians and actors in the systemic approach.

Dualistic approaches, like those found in Karl Marx's work, see society as the struggle between two opposing but necessarily interlocked groups, classes, or forces. In Marx's theory it was the conflict between the capitalist class and the workers who had no control over the means of production. The secret of societal inquiry is to locate the fundamental opposition or contradiction in society that is driving its processes. In Marx this approach took a revolutionary turn to resolve the contradiction. In conservative dualisms, the opposition is permanent, whether between the elite and the masses or the supreme race and the enslaved race. Indeed, as in the history of Soviet and Chinese Communism, the seemingly revolutionary class can simply transform itself into such a permanent ruling class. The dualism persists but in a different form.

Pluralistic approaches see society as a constantly changing collection of groups vying for power. Changing technologies, environmental conditions, or even ideological developments yield constant fluctuations in the relationships of these various groups. This perspective has often figured in the work of American political scientists and theorists, for they see it reflecting the usual state of affairs in our political history.

Finally, we turned this ideal-type analysis of approaches to the discipline of personality, delineating them as Conflict, Equilibrium, and Fulfillment approaches. The conflict approach to the self has a long history from St. Paul and St. Augustine to Martin Luther and Sigmund Freud. In this approach the self is constituted by a struggle between competing forces, whether they be seen as reason and passion, flesh and spirit, or ego and id. The conflict is never resolved but takes varying forms throughout our life. Therapy seeks to help us live more functionally or with less disturbance but it can never remove these underlying conflicts. They make us who we are.

Equilibrium approaches see the self as a rough balance among inner forces and our environment. Most behaviorists are found here, since they see the self as the outcome of responses to stimuli, both negative and positive, from their environment. Therapies that emphasize changing our behaviors, thinking, and reactions to our environment reflect an equilibrium approach.

Fulfillment approaches see the self as emerging from the struggle of an inner "true self" to break out of various impediments, whether internal or external, that constrict its expression of its inner dynamism. The humanist psychologists, such as Carl Rogers and Abraham Maslow, reflect this approach. Rather than the self being the product of an intractable conflict, this approach sees the self as an evolving unity seeking the fulfillment of its basic needs. Maslow, with his hierarchy of needs-fulfillment, typifies this approach.

Connecting the Disciplines: The Triads

Once we had roughly sorted out these distinct strains in the three disciplines, we began to explore how an approach in one discipline, say ecstatic

Christianity, might have a preference, an "elective affinity," as Max Weber would have called it, to a particular approach in society and personality. As we worked through the literature in these fields we came to the hypothesis of "primary triads" and "secondary triads" of approaches. In a box form, which characterizes much of my earlier work, it looks like this:

PRIMARY INTERDISCIPLINARY TRIADS		
CHRISTIANITY	SOCIETY	PERSONALITY
Cultic	Systemic	Conflict
Prophetic	Dualist	Equilibrium
Ecstatic	Pluralist	Fulfillment

Why do these approaches tend to stick together? In exploring this question we characteristically led out from the Christian approaches to their bias toward the others.

The Cultic Primary Triad

A cultic Christianity focuses on the symbols, rituals, and sacraments of the church. It has usually been tied to a systemic theory of society because a social system finds its long-term stability in a coherent cultural grounding of symbols and rituals—its cultic core—that unites all its members in a common orientation. Having been formed in this basic unifying culture, the members can then exercise their various functions with a large degree of seeming independence and autonomy and with a minimum of coercion. The role of the church in classic European and English society immediately comes to mind. It was the dominant model of church and society relations borne by the Roman Catholic tradition in which I was immersed in those years. In order to deal with the tensions that may arise among members who do not fit in according to the culture, this triad then turns to conflict psychology and internalizes social conflicts inside the self.

Sigmund Freud's *Civilization and its Discontents* beautifully illustrates this move. What would be social conflict in pluralistic and dualistic approaches to society is seen more as an internal and perpetual conflict in the self, something that cannot be ameliorated by changes in the society. The society and its allied church provide symbolic means as well as institutions to help selves process these conflicts but they cannot resolve them in this life.

The Prophetic Primary Triad

Prophetic Christians, with their focus on the objective moral plumb line by which God evaluates and seeks to redeem and perfect our lives, are drawn to the dualistic approach in society because this approach contains within it a sense of intractable conflict between the dominant and the suppressed classes, races, or strata of society. This instability arises because the construction of the society violates some outside, transcendent norms for proper ordering of human life. To preserve the social arrangement increasing amounts of coercion are required. The contradictions or warfare of a society are illuminated by taking a stand outside of the strain toward internal stability characteristic of the systemic approach.

This prophetic-dualist combination can be revolutionary as well as deeply conservative. If Christian moral commitments require the existence of an elite to constrain the ignorance or moral deviance of the subordinate group, then a prophetic approach requires maintaining the dualism as a necessity of faith. If the prophetic stance sees an ideal beyond the present order, such as the "kingdom of God" or the "New Heaven and the New Earth," it may seek to trace out the ways the dualism will be overcome in some radical way. Here we see the difference between the authoritarianism of traditional Latin American society, governed by Church and aristocracy, and the liberation theology of someone like Gustavo Gutierrez, whose work we explored in the book.

The prophetic dualist then usually turns to an equilibrium approach to personality because personality change emerges not from a struggle with the intractable conflicts of the self or a trust in the internal drive to individual fulfillment, but from accommodation to the right order that is embedded in the very will of God—in God's law and Torah. In secular language this order may be called "natural law" or "ecological equilibrium." This law and these ethical precepts need to be taught by those who have grasped them, whether through rational inquiry or revealed insight. This higher law needs to penetrate the reason and shape the will. This is the thrust of every utopian Christian community we knew as well as more traditional Christian sects and the *communidades de base* of liberation theology. It has its secular counterparts in the Marxist and socialist utopianism of the nineteenth century and the Communist cadres of the twentieth.

The Ecstatic Primary Triad

Ecstatic Christians tend to prefer pluralistic approaches to society because their emphasis on the expressive capacities of the individual predisposes them to voluntary associations that can take many different forms. Moreover, in order to enable this flowering of individual spirits, power in a society must be decentralized to make room for a variety of alternative social forms. Just as in Christianity the emphasis on individual experience and conscience led to a pluralism of Christian sects and churches, now called denominations, so its social partner is a pluralism of associations, parties, publics, and states. The completion of this triad with a fulfillment psychology should be fairly obvious, since both emphasize the priority of personal experience and expression. Both church and voluntary associations emerge as arenas for the nurture and expression of the true self generated by personal encounters with the Spirit of God.

The Secondary Triads

In spite of these primary affinities among approaches in the three disciplines, their differing loyalties, practices, and theories still create tensions within these alliances, even as there are perennial tensions among the approaches within a discipline. These intractable tensions among the three disciplines, we came to realize, frequently tend to push each primary triad to a secondary set of connections. In cultic Christianity, the tight bond between cultic and systemic approaches can take on a different personality approach. Rather than choose a conflict approach, which internalizes social conflict within the self, a cultic approach may, when it finds itself in a more harmonious setting, take on a fulfillment approach to the person. It emphasizes a smoother connection between the internal expressive needs of the self and the Christian and societal disciplines in which it lives. The Thomistic synthesis of theology and social theory that has dominated modern Catholic social theory reflects this kind of move.

In prophetic Christianity, we find a different move regarding the location of conflict. While maintaining the prophetic-dualist connection, prophetic Christians, because of the pastoral experience of dealing with people's perennial personal struggles, may shift from an equilibrium approach to the person to a conflict approach. In a sense, this simply heightens the sense of conflict, placing it both in society and in the self. The result may be an eventual move to a fuller cultic and systemic choice—the cultic primary triad—which postpones the resolution of the societal conflict into a more distant and perhaps more apocalyptic future.

Ecstatic Christianity, because it is least concerned with the shape of the society around the person, can move away from its usual choice of social pluralism to embrace both a dualistic and a systemic connection. Just as the systemic approach to society can take on a fulfillment approach to the person, so can its usual Christian partner, ecstatic Christianity, choose a systemic partner. With a dualistic choice, which is the least frequent, ecstatic Christianity can look for the overthrow of all social inequalities and oppressions, releasing the self into a wide-ranging anarchy in which justice and harmony arise purely from the good will of fully expressive persons. On the other hand, ecstatic Christianity could choose a systemic approach that sees the full flowering of the self in a harmonious social system.

While we assume that ecstatic Christianity will almost always choose a fulfillment approach to personality, in some cases it may take up some of the themes in a conflict approach to personality. In this case, the conflicts within the self are overcome by the incursion of the Holy Spirit, which finally subdues or transforms the self-destructive aspects of the self, releasing the true self to a higher life of freedom. This seems to have been the path taken by St. Paul in the church's earliest days.

Thus, while the primary triads arise from strong and persistent strains within each approach, there are numerous ways that other choices can be made. However, the primary triads have a stability and logical consistency that continually draw secondary triads to resolve back into a primary triad. I did not reflect at the time on the way that this volatility among the triads is usually due to changes in the personality partner of a triad. From this later vantage point I think we could have pointed out ways that Christian approaches might also move from one to another societal partner, bringing along a personality partner in its wake. I think it may be, however, that the link between the institutional church and a societal partner is more stable simply because of the power dynamics at work, while personality is a much more variable part of human life.

The triadic patterns raise questions for anyone, asking why certain moves have been taken, what tendencies need to be accounted for, and where points of change and strain will arise as people knit together their approaches to Christianity, personality, and society. The triadic hypothesis sets up the framework for arguments about the various ways of putting together the relationships of Christianity to possible societal and personality partners. Because of this framework's complexity, we even played with the fantasy of making it into a board game. Maybe it could become a competitor for Dungeons and Dragons! Alas, our academic seriousness short-circuited such playfulness. My son, however, went into a career in which he led elaborate mystery games for eager conferees and employees of large institutions. Some things have to await their generation.

In this retrospective presentation of the main outlines of *Disciplines*, it is impossible to review the numerous authors that we used as case studies or examples. Carl Rogers, Saul Alinsky, Thomas Oden, and Gustavo Gutierrez received special attention. Almost every page bears reference to some relevant figures in theology or the behavioral sciences, many of them now fading from our awareness. It was a rich conversation dependent on our exploration of a wide range of figures who had shaped our thought and action in particular ways.

Yet we were not through with our task by drawing out the structure of relationships among the dimensions of theory, practice and loyalty and among the approaches in the three disciplines. The next section of *Disciplines* was devoted to working out the questions that we bundled under the concept of congruence among loyalties, theories, and practices.

Congruence

Concern with what we called congruence arises because each approach consists of practices as well as theories and loyalties. These approaches are not merely abstract "isms." They are ways of living in history and cultural context. All of us struggle with the question of what practices fit our loyalties. What ways of thinking about the world are most suited for changing it in accordance with our loyalties? What theories actually lead to the practices we have developed? How we fit these three dimensions together in our personal and institutional lives is a question thoughtful people encounter every day. It lies at the heart of ethics as well as intellectual integrity and trustworthy relationships with others.

My deep interest in this problem may have reflected my own struggle to find the practices that might mesh with (and not just flow from) the intensely idealistic intellectual constructs I had worked out in my first thirty years. It was an explicit form of my struggle for inner as well as public integrity. It was a step in the movement from exploring the infinite variety of existence to becoming a more vital actor within it and its constraints.

Simple Congruence

To explore this problem we distinguished between simple congruence and functional congruence. Simple congruence points first of all to a logical fit among the dimensions of practice, theory, and loyalty within an approach. If we prioritize, as Carl Rogers did, the key value of the autonomy of the self, then we have to be careful in our practice about conveying judgments, whether by the therapist, by the practices we promote, or by a group gathered for therapy. If we shift anything in our practice, we must also take account of it with shifts in our theory and even our loyalties. This is true of all the disciplines.

The second type of simple congruence arises among disciplines. How is it fitting for a priest in a cultic approach to Christianity to choose a pluralistic or even dualistic approach to society, rather than the customary systemic approach? Gustavo Gutierrez was noted for his choice of a strongly dualistic (Marxist) approach to society. To do so, he had to emphasize the importance of the Bible's prophetic tradition. Priests involved in Alinsky-style community organization, as was wide-spread in the Milwaukee and Chicago of our environment at the time, had to make similar adjustments in order to be congruent in their choice of other disciplinary practices, theories, and loyalties.

Functional Congruence

The demand of functional congruence asks us to inquire into how a practice, theory, or loyalty actually functions in a specific historical and cultural context. This is not only a demand by the behavioral sciences but also a demand arising in the historic Christian (as well as Jewish and Muslim) concern for the way our well-intentioned acts of worship or ethical behavior may actually function in an idolatrous or sinful way. As we were writing we were becoming acutely aware of the way Western Christianity had justified slavery, racism, and oppression of women by the kinds of songs, texts, preaching, ecclesiastical practice, and symbols of God and Jesus we had used in our history.

The Christian problem of idolatry is analogous to the concept of ideology in social science, introduced in Germany by Karl Mannheim and later developed by the Frankfurt School in the 1930s. Ideology is a set of seemingly descriptive ideas or symbols that actually functions to mask or reinforce the underlying realities of a society. Invoking the free market and capitalism to mask the actual centralized power of large corporations is one example. In other contexts, claiming that a centralized oligarchy is the workers' party would be another.

This slip between a seemingly descriptive concept and its use in a prescriptive way that disguises reality is also evident in psychological theories that seem to describe the development of the self, say in stages or ages, and the notion (a loyalty) that we should proceed in this particular way, going from a "lower" to a "higher" mode of functioning. In all of these cases, functional congruence is more than a matter of being a logical fit but of how an idea, practice, or loyalty actually affects human activity.

All of these discussions of congruence rest on an underlying commitment to a particular view of what reality is, whether it be societal, psychological, or theological. We see this in contests over what is really causing the anguish individuals experience in their lives. Theologically, of course, we tend to be even more aware of this competition over what God "really is" or is "really doing." And of course, we see it again in contests over what is really causing the conflicts, malfunctions, or inequalities in society.

Finally, each discipline sees itself as having privileged knowledge of what is really real, whether it be psychological, sociological, or theological. Each discipline tends to interpret the claims of the other in terms of its own and to have a more basic grasp of what is important, what is real, and what is really operative in our lives. This tendency of each discipline to reduce the others to its own framework leads us from the mapping of disciplines, dimensions, and approaches, each with its own issues of congruence, to the final task—understanding the activity of critique and transformation among the disciplines, a task which gave the book its name. In this negotiation among the disciplines we are all pushed to define one of them as our "homeland," where our fundamental loyalties and perspectives lie. At this point the methodological dance of the book was pushing me to define more clearly where I would commit my time and energy. While this life-long work continues, it is also clear that I was constructing a more adequate way to carry the Christian passport in my professional and personal life.

The Critical Task of Interdisciplinary Transformation

Our final step was to map the outcomes of this engagement among approaches to Christianity, society, and personality. These outcomes arise from both formal and substantive criticisms among these partners. Formal criticism demands that we put each option through the criticisms shaped by the trilateral map—checking for congruence, coherence, integrity and clarity about the reality around us. Substantive criticism is driven by a loyalty to a particular set of approaches and their accompanying practices, theories, and loyalties. It finally has to decide that not all approaches have the same validity.

We continually move back and forth between these two forms of criticism as we deepen and enlarge our repertoire of practices, theories, and loyalties. At various points we arrive at a standpoint for sorting out claims about the realities we have recognized and the way we might wish to change them. We may arrive at a point where the prophetic triad and its partners seem most convincing for charting our way ahead. Or we may come to the conclusion that a conflict psychology, with its partners, best orients us to the world and its possible transformation.

This process of criticism by means of trilateral analysis leads us to six possible outcomes. One is to simply reject some elements of other approaches or partners in the exchange. At the very least, we put some element in the engagement at the bottom of our list. Sometimes we might reject a partner outright, as in an atheistic rejection of any Christian approach from the standpoint of a societal approach. While some rejections are important to developing a strong position, we found this the least satisfying.

We also may simply add an element to our substantive position, as when we incorporate a therapeutic practice into a pastoral counseling repertoire. Such an addition automatically raises questions about possible necessary changes in other aspects of one's overall position, so it is usually only a first step. Otherwise, we become eclectic tourists without any coherent program of action or thought.

When we construct very strong loyalties around a particular set of approaches we often engage in a reduction of the others to our own approach. This leads to the "nothing but" of reducing a Christian theory to a psychological one, or a societal perspective to a theological struggle between good and evil. At this point the trilateral exchange itself is jeopardized.

A more positive response is an outcome we called corroboration, in which another approach is a confirmation of what we have already come to embrace. In this case the other approach does not lead to any critical questions about our own, but we do not reduce it to our own. Its possible critiques simply lie dormant.

Corroboration can become a more active relationship when we translate that approach into our own. Therapy is translated into salvation, the soul into the psyche, or alienation into sin. Mission is translated as revolution or therapeutic self-expression as confession.

Finally, after working through this thicket of outcomes, we lifted up that of transformation, indeed reciprocal transformation. We may retain many of our original substantive commitments but they have been changed under the impact of the trilateral exchange. Moreover, we may have introduced some transformation into our conversation partner in the other disciplines. Just as our pastoral counseling may have embraced a more complex approach to personalities, so therapists in the realm of personality may have a deeper understanding of the way theologies have plumbed depths of suffering and longing that they may have overlooked. Reciprocal transformation was put forth as the most important outcome of the trilateral framework and conversation we had developed.

The Cabinet and the Contents

In setting forth this bare-boned architecture of the trilateral analysis in *Disciplines in Transformation* I have given scant attention to the people inhabiting these rooms and corridors. The book itself is chock-a-block with the figures and movements that shaped people's thought and practice, indeed their loyalties, at the time. As I look back I see how much it was a work of cabinetry with which to organize my professional world, even though I have not had space here to lift out much of the contents. It was a work of mapping out the world I was committed to working in as a professional theological educator grounded in the disciplines of Christian ethics. It also laid out some of the ways I might think critically about these relationships and ways of thinking about and acting in the world. However, even though I was often embroiled in the social change efforts of the sixties and seventies I had not yet really laid out a substantive position that might have better guided these involvements.

However, the work of mapping out the interdisciplinary conversation was a substantive commitment in itself. In trying to frame a map for this engagement I was giving voice to themes that began in my early life in Washington. It was, if you will, a work of diplomacy and interdisciplinary statecraft that fleshed out not only a particular interdisciplinary conversation but also the process of conversation and argument that led much later to my commitment to "reconciling conversations" and restorative justice. It required respect for the integrity of the other, an effort to hold together our wider loyalties with our thinking and acting, as well as an openness to transformation in the process. Like real-world diplomacy, it had no fixed end point but sought to establish working coalitions to deal with problems that beset a common world. While we laid out some of the theological bases for this set of methodological commitments, I did not fully understand or explore them at the time.

My life was being shaped not only by the tumult of those years, but also by the worship and work of my Roman Catholic colleagues in Milwaukee and beyond. So deeply was I engaged in Catholic life that many people, including Gregory Baum, simply assumed I was a Catholic lay theologian. I was well on my way to the "ecumaniac" title I took for myself in subsequent years.

At the same time, the confluence of my Baptist, Episcopalian, and Catholic streams was augmented by work with the Study Commission of the Lutheran World Federation. Thanks to my friend Gerd Decke, I was asked by its Director, Ulrich Duchrow, to be a consultant to the LWF's effort to deal with the pluralism of church institutions and conceptions of their mission in the various cultures in which Lutheran churches found themselves in the post-war years.[1] From 1975 to 1977 I spent time in Geneva, Switzerland, and Heidelberg, Germany, reflecting on case studies generated by various church groups in Africa, India, the United States, Latin America, and Europe to discern ways that Lutheran theological tradition could be held together with an increasing pluralism of institutional and programmatic forms. This case study method continued to inform me in

---

1. Lutheran World Federation, *Identity of the Church*.

subsequent years, especially in the studies that constituted my later work on federalism, religion, and public life.

While Tim Bachmeyer and I were bringing a final form to the method presented in *Disciplines in Transformation*, I turned this critical lens on myself and my professional association, the Society of Christian Ethics. In a paper for the Society's annual meeting in 1976 I sought to clarify what was at stake in the debate between ethicists who wanted to be engaged in action for social change and those who saw the discipline of ethics as more reflective and removed from immediate strategic concerns. The essay was subsequently published as "Vocation and Location: An Exploration in the Ethics of Ethics," in *The Journal of Religious Ethics*.

Lifting up the social theories (the "approaches") implicit in the activists' and reflectionists' views of an ethicist's vocation, I examined their differing views of power and authority. Adoption of either of these approaches was in turn shaped by the primary social location of ethicists in higher education and church agencies, as well as their secondary locations in voluntary associations and, in a few cases, corporations. Finally, I examined what the profession as such should do as it sought to clarify ethical choices as well as promote visions of the right and good congruent with and essential to its own existence. I argued for a mix of social locations for ethicists as well as a focus on pluralistic approaches in social theory. The essay "presented the vocation of ethics as a task, not only of reflection, but also of participation in a variety of social locations."[2] As such, it expressed my own search for a clearer vocational path that implemented the method of trilateral analysis and also moved me to substantive social and ethical commitments.

Even as I was working out the diplomatic practices for connecting all these strands of theology, ecclesiology, and cultural life, several events in my personal life were pushing me to deepen and clarify my substantive commitments. One was the steady decline and loss of my family's farm in Virginia. The other was the decline and disintegration of my marriage.

---

2. Everett, "Vocation and Location," 109.

III

COMMITMENTS AND CONVICTIONS

Land Ethics

IN THE COURSE OF the nineteen-seventies, it became increasingly clear that my family's dairy farm in Loudoun County, Virginia, was becoming economically unviable. Washington's expansion was driving up land prices, equipment costs were rising, and the farm families were growing older while their children were migrating to the cities. Moreover, because of fleets of refrigerated tank trucks bringing Wisconsin's milk into the hitherto legally protected "milksheds" of the Maryland-Virginia area, milk prices remained flat. (Indeed, even as a student at Wesleyan I had written a paper on milk-pricing systems and dairy cooperatives.) We were running out of string to tie the operation together. And, of course, I was one of those who had left home for a career that would never enable me to take up my father's role as he had done with his father.

These pressures, which weighed heavily on my father, drove me to deeper reflection about one crucial component of this disintegrating web of life—land. The land trust movement and its conservationist allies were gaining increasing visibility as a way to enable farm families to remain on the land, just as the leasehold system in Britain had preserved much of their farmland. Though families did not "own" the land there in fee simple, they could farm it generation after generation. Since I was now living in the very state whose milk was threatening the survival of our farm, I was in an environment where land issues found ready resonance among some of my students, although one of them claimed to be uninterested in land issues, "because I plan to have an urban ministry." Undaunted, I plowed ahead with my interest in the form of research that led to a paper I presented to the Society of Christian Ethics in January 1979 entitled "Land Ethics: Toward a Covenantal Model."

While the article reflected the style of mapping I was completing in *Disciplines*, it developed its own grid and led to a specific commitment to a covenantal framework. First, it identified four parties making claims on the land: God, Nature, Society, and Persons. This formal categorization already reflected the covenantal framework of negotiation, agreement, and claims to promises made by parties to the biblical covenant. As seen through the prism of Israel's testimonies, God, the first partner, is both creator of the land and also the source of Israel's habitation on the land, conditioned by its own keeping of God's covenant for its proper care.

"Nature" comprises all the natural processes of the land's physical life. It is the "ecological system," as we were coming to recognize it. As I understood the ecological perspective at that time, "Nature is a moving equilibrium of forces and processes striving for harmony."[1] The natural "laws" of this dynamic process, as we are now seeing with relentless climate change, have their own inevitable claim on the land. For a society, land constitutes not only the physical basis for its survival but also yields up conditions and events, such as topography, climate, earthquakes and storm patterns, that shape the very ethos and culture of a people. It is a theater for the drama of a society's history. It can gain a sacredness of its own.

"Society" points to "the total complex of human relations laying claim to the land." In this formulation, it "embraces the whole complex of activities by which people sustain themselves." Through specific institutions, governments, and organizations societies act in a unified way to maintain or create various ways of managing land and the disputes over it. This was a markedly systemic and organic conception of society, even though the whole approach to land ethics I took reflected my more enduring pluralistic stance.

Finally, I drew on my earlier work on the concept of the person to single out the individual and corporate entities that societies recognize as having valid claims on the land. Corporate persons include not only private organizations but also public ones like governments as well as trusts and

---

1. Everett, "Land Ethics," 47.

cooperatives. In American history and culture, the idea of persons, usually representing whole families, "owning" the land was the bedrock of the yeoman farmer ideal espoused by Thomas Jefferson, albeit in slave-holding plantation style. The presence in American history of many people deprived of personhood was a theme I would only start unpacking in my later work. That corporate persons could also be state actors was somewhat of a conceptual confusion I didn't address in this paper, since I was concerned with articulating a certain covenantal perspective that I had not worked on earlier.

Each of these parties can and does make differing claims on the land, claims that are often in conflict with one another. How, then, should we understand these conflicts and the paths toward their resolution, even if any arrangement among them is both tentative and temporary?

These four parties can lay claim to certain rights regarding the land. By exercising these rights the parties can seek a range of goods. Recognition of the legitimate rights among the parties then yields up a set of obligations they bear to one another. Examining this web of rights, goods, and obligations is a typical problem for ethicists. I began by listing four rights that can be related to the land.

Ownership is in reality a bundle of rights that can be separated out from one another. I identified them as use, income, transfer, and alteration. Use entails occupancy or some kind of exploitation of the land through agriculture, hunting, or some kind of commerce.

Related to exploitation is the more indirect right to income. Thus, someone may not actually work the land but have a right to some or all of its produce through some legal or commercial transaction. Taxes are an income that a society, through its government, may extract from the land.

The right to transfer other rights to the land to another party is in itself a distinct right. We can only transfer the rights we already have, however. A society may constrain what rights can be transferred. One of the most interesting developments for me at the time was the notion that people could transfer the right to alter the land to some permanent legal entity.

This final right I called alteration rather than the customary "development" in order to avoid the notion that a more intense market-driven use of the land improved it ecologically. The conservation movement has increasingly used this transfer of alteration rights to preserve farmland or land of particular beauty or ecological importance.

I then turned to the identification of the goods that the various parties seek to secure through the exercise of their rights with regard to the land. Keep in mind that I was trying to broaden the discussion from the usual focus on persons and society to include Nature (the ecological system) and God, the Creator. Obviously, the attention to God was grounded in the biblical traditions informing our culture and gave me entrée into wider theological concerns as well. The four goods I identified were security, expression, enjoyment, and perfection.

Security entails both survival as well as sustainability of the land, regardless of which partners are benefitted. Nature, we think, instinctually struggles to sustain itself in a moving equilibrium of forces. Individuals, families, and societies do the same. Expression can refer to God's expression of the divine power and beauty through the creation. The same can be said of nature's expression in ecological processes. Societies express key values through their approach to land use, whether it is reconfiguring the land for the purpose of transportation, the building of monuments, or particular patterns of urban design and agriculture. And, of course, individuals seek to express their values in the way they use or alter the land as well as transfer its control, especially to their offspring.

Enjoyment, which I acknowledged as a peculiar good, is the reciprocal good of expression. We seek to enjoy land for the goods it gives us, but we can also enjoy it in a way that simply receives what is innate in the land, whether it be beauty, air, spiritual growth, awesome grandeur, or solitude. This is the good underlying much of our effort to conserve wilderness, parks, and other land features from the claims of other parties on it for use, income or alteration.

Finally, perfection is the good that a party seeks in the land in order to realize its ultimate purpose. Here I turned again to the way Israel's land and its flourishing was to be the realization of God's aim for the earth. At various points in this essay I acknowledged the importance of process theology and Whitehead's philosophy on my fundamental outlook. The idea that life on this earth is part of a transcendent process through which God realizes the divine purpose was nurtured throughout my college and graduate work by extensive study of the thought of Alfred North Whitehead, Charles Hartshorne, and the "process school" of philosophers and theologians. While it reflected the implicit Calvinism of my upbringing, it turned away from the rigidly mechanical and deterministic framework it had taken on in the age of Descartes and Newton.

Perfection can also be attributed to nature's drive toward its own sustainable equilibrium. With regard to persons and societies, perfection can be seen as the explication of the good of expression drawn out to its greatest extent. Of course, the perfection sought by a yeoman farmer and the perfection sought by a multinational corporation are drastically different and even contradictory! In this respect, I now see that the listing of these goods, while introducing important considerations for a covenantal land ethics, was more strained than it needed to be. My substantive commitments were pushing at the limits of a rigorous formal scheme. However, it has always been very important to me to find some way of organizing the actual complexity of the world and of the ethical challenges we face in acting in it. This reflects the ongoing struggle between my diplomatic and prophetic commitments.

Out of this grid of four parties, four rights, and four goods I then constructed four ethical models. (I know there could have been more!) They were a market model, a societal model, an ecological model, and a covenantal model. The market model is the dominant model in American life. Most land is simple governed by its capacity to be put into a market governed by the exchange power of money. Many laws favor the "highest and best use" of land in monetary and market terms for governing how society assigns land use, income, and alteration.

Without an extensive argument, I pointed out the limitations of this model, mainly because it ends up restricting all other parties and goods from consideration. People have always turned to societal organizations to limit the play of the market. This societal model then introduces the rights of nature, society, and even God. When some form of society enters to counteract the dominance of the market, it may become very collectivist or may also be very traditionalist. Political processes or communal traditions may counteract market forces. Unfortunately, these societal models can simply replace the concentrations of power created by the market with other concentrations of power. Neither need respect the claims of nature or of God.

This concern gives rise to an ecological model in which the ecological system is to govern how land is held and used. At a practical level, it is scientists of that system—geologists, ecologists, agronomists, and the like—who shape these decisions and policies. In this model it is nature's expression and perfection that is to be maximized. The other parties yield to these demands, ultimately for their own good. However, it is often difficult to discern how the goods of the other parties are to be realized. Nature usually changes too slowly to reveal the consequences of our actions. Climate change, which was barely on the horizon for me at the time, is our most cogent and pervasive example today. If there is any proof for natural law, it should be the inexorable way that climate change resulting from human activity is imperiling the very survival of the human race and many other species that share our delicate state of equilibrium. While very important, this model's limitations led me to flesh out a covenantal model rooted more in biblical traditions and the more specific ethics it can yield.

"In the Covenantal model God is the primary party and the land is a trust God established with His people."[2] Working from this claim meant that each of God's creatures was to have a share in the land and its benefits. Nature itself is not a machine with discrete replaceable parts but a unity permeated with God's purpose. Flowing from this conception are derivative rights for the various parties to the land, but all are to be referred back to the Creator's own purposes.

While this short article could not explore this model in detail, it could identify some leads I would take later. First of all, it highlighted the roles of persons and societies as trustees and stewards of the land. This was a value always emphasized by my father, even as his capacity to exercise this trusteeship was being swallowed up by market forces. Secondly, it sought to tie together markets, social and governmental institutions, and the ecological system into a theologically-grounded framework. At the end of the article I pointed to the land trust movement as a promising vehicle for realizing this more interdependent and sustainable model for land policy and practices. As I look back on it now, this little article, with its covenantal and ecological emphases, set up much of the agenda that occupied the next ten or fifteen years of my intellectual and public life.

Stewardship Ethics

Within a few months of presenting this paper I was invited to a conference on stewardship ethics sponsored by Pax Christi, a noted Catholic social action organization. In my contribution I presented a re-thinking of the famous stewardship parable, "The Parable of the Talents," in Matthew's Gospel, chapter 25. First, I pointed out how the concept of stewardship draws us to the use of things, while trusteeship draws us to their ownership.

2. Everett, "Land Ethics," 62.

Stewardship has generally focused our attention in an individualistic manner, while trusteeship opens up wider communal and societal dimensions. It was these wider concerns that drove my interpretation of the parable.

The "talent" which the steward is entrusted with in the parable was simply a unit of money in Jesus's world. However, the parable itself gave rise to the notion that "talent," first in Latin and then in English, meant a God-given ability, usually an ability to make money. However, more expansively, it meant an ability given to us through which we can glorify God. It was this interpretation that powerfully legitimated the rise of an occupational business society in the sixteenth to nineteenth centuries. Who has not been told that they must discover and exercise the talent God has given them? Piano teachers, I smiled, have certainly benefitted from this admonition. (I, however, thought I had other talents to find. Chemistry, I recall, took precedence over the music my mother urged me to. I never did become a chemist, but I have been singing ever since. Little boys hate to think that their mothers might be right in something!)

This individualistic, market-oriented interpretation, I argued, is misguided if not wrong. If "talent" in this parable is a metaphor, we need to look at it in the context of the parables about faithful bridesmaids, servants, and charity that surround it. All of them, I argued, are about fidelity to the Gospel. The "talent" in the parable is the Gospel itself. The Gospel is a message and way of life given to us by God through Jesus that we share with others in service to God's mission of salvation. This is a communal task of building up the community of the saints, to whom the Gospel is entrusted. The parable is about the multiplying of faith in service to the Gospel and the community that is entrusted with it. In this way the parable moves from its individualistic function of legitimating market-place occupations to a communitarian work of sharing faith and trust. It emphasizes cooperation rather than competition, the good of all rather than strictly personal goods.

I then moved to the emphasis on holding the Gospel "in trust," which runs through the New Testament, as in I Corinthians 9:17 and I Timothy 1:11. Through the conception of trust, I turned the parable back to the stewardship of the land that had guided my father's own efforts. But what is a trust? I spelled out this concept in terms of the classic formulations of the "settler" of the trust, the trustees, the property of the trust, the beneficiaries, and the instrument by which the trust is implemented.

God is the settler, or establisher, of the trust in which we inhabit the land, as in the Genesis story as well as in the "giving" of the land to Abraham, something which I see as a trusteeship to Israel and not a gift. This trusteeship requires a covenant among the trustees about the administration of the trust, whose property ultimately belongs to God. In my formulation, this position of trusteeship was entered into by all those who share in this faith in God as Creator.

In calling the earth God's property entrusted to us, I expanded the notion of the Latin *proprium* so that the land is really "proper" to God as God's means of expression and perfection. Through it we really encounter the divine purpose, power, and beauty.

The beneficiaries of this trust are all future generations. Here I neglected to include all other creatures, indeed the eco-system as such. That was a limitation on my understanding at the time, something I shared with a lot of people, of course, but no less glaring in retrospect. To spell out the implications of this broader understanding was a very complex task I would have to address later.

In describing the instrument of this trust I rehearsed the various rights to the land from my recent article. This led back to an emphasis on the land trust idea as a way to speak of the trusteeship in the parable as well as the stewardship of the Gospel (the "talent") that God entrusts to us.

This understanding of the parable has of course caused my teeth to grind as I sat through typical sermons on it over the past thirty-plus years. However, it has remained central to my reconstruction of the parable in an ecological, covenantal, and ecclesiological perspective.

The Hinge of Personal Transformation

Just as I entered into this more substantive critical work stimulated by concern for ecology and public life, my private life was taking a drastic turn. My own marriage, founded more in care-taking and life-construction than in conjugal love and intimacy, had come to a point of exhaustion. It had indeed become a work of diplomacy and negotiation, but it could not resolve my deep search for a more adequate relationship. In 1980 I entered into divorce from my wife of fifteen years. This was a struggle over my own identity, my roles in life, and the meaning of covenant, grace, forgiveness, and the energies of love. As one of my closest friends said at the time, I began to be shaped by a search for integrity, not only within my emotional life, but in my spirituality as well. My subsequent life of love and marriage with Sylvia, now my wife of thirty-eight years, has been rich in sharing and collaboration, both personally and professionally. The profound experiences of these years transformed my theology as well as my life and relationships in numerous ways.

In this time of personal change we became members of the United Methodist Church, which appealed to my search for a more expansive ecclesiology, a richer sense of worship, and a strong social ethic. As one sign of this transition, I took Sylvia's family name as my middle name, as she took my family name for her last name, when we married in a ceremony with two Catholic priests and our Methodist minister. At the time we were active in a racially mixed Catholic parish as well as our white Methodist congregation. The fusion of African American music and spirit with Catholic liturgy has informed our own spirituality ever since. As this transformation played out in my private life, it began to shape my public life and work. In some sense it set much of the trajectory for my work ever since.

God's Federal Republic

My work on civil religion with Robert Bellah and my subsequent years at St. Francis Seminary had led me to an ongoing reflection on the meaning of symbols and rituals for ethics, church order, and social structure. I kept returning in those reflections to the dissonance between the inherited religious symbols of kingdom, monarchy, lordship, patriarchy, and family order and our actual commitments to democracy within a constitutional republic. The symbolic world of most Christian worship was either far removed from the world of political commitments I shared with my fellow citizens or it was a reactionary threat to them.

In addition, my substantive commitments to a pluralistic societal approach had been strengthened by my embrace of more elements of an ecstatic approach to Christian faith in those years. My struggle for a more fulfilling personal life could not be confined to a prophetic Christian commitment to marital duty or covenant without the power of unitive love. This meant that I was increasingly at odds with the theological framework and cultic forms I had inherited as a Protestant Christian. Patriarchal care and control could not be the paradigm for my worship any more than it could be for my private as well as public life. However, rather than rejecting the prophetic strains that had accented my judgmental stance in society, I could mine them for a fuller appropriation of the ways my covenantal heritage was grounded in the ecstatic experience of God's love and grace.

Commitments and Convictions

The writings of Jonathan Edwards, John Milton, Roger Williams (a distant ancestor), and many other Puritan and Independent thinkers augmented this connection.

At the same time as this realignment and re-appropriation in my life and thought was occurring in the early nineteen-eighties, I also encountered another wrenching change. While I had often entertained notions of moving to a different institution for my work, my divorce had committed me to remaining in Milwaukee in order to help care for my children. However, a new, much more traditional Pope was sending a chill through the Roman Catholic Church about the kind of work I and many others had been engaged in. Moreover, the Seminary, like other Catholic institutions, was encountering financial problems as the post-war religious bubble and the ethnic cultures that had sustained it began to wane. In spite of my rank and longevity, my appointment was terminated. Though a number of loyal colleagues jumped in to ensure a proper severance, the effort to hold together my newly-won Catholic sensibilities and relationships with my historic Protestant commitments and perspectives was deeply shaken.

In the midst of this personal upheaval I began to craft a book that would reconstruct the symbols of Christian worship in ways that could engage the world of constitutional republicanism and democracy deep in my marrow. I called it "God's Federal Republic." In it I re-visioned the symbol of "Kingdom of God" that I had been raised on by my Social Gospel precursors through the lens of my inherited American political and cultural experience. I wrote the first draft in the autumn of 1984, while I worked in the limbo between my previous employment and the hoped-for new landing where I could once again deploy my professional energies. While the wrenching dissociation from my Catholic world of teaching and research heightened my distrust of the patriarchy embedded in Catholic tradition, I carried with me a Catholic commitment to cultural engagement, to the importance of ecclesiology, and to the conciliar traditions that had re-emerged in the work of the Second Vatican Council. All of these figured in the deep commitments of this emerging work.

This reconstruction was forged as an alternative to the principal political visions that were competing for our attention after World War II. Marxism, while providing a wide-ranging critique of capitalism, could not provide a political vision grounded in human rights, voluntary association, pluralism, and political negotiation. The neo-conservative movements of the day could not conceive of a common good other than the simple outcome of the pursuit of private or, as it has emerged, ethnic self-interest. Both relegated religion to the private sphere without any critical engagement with the public realm, seeking only to use it as an instrument of their own political objectives. Finally, the fundamentalist movements of the day, both reactionary and utopian, tended to fuse religion and politics into some theocratic patriarchal vision that also eliminated genuine politics and a vigorous public life.

My work in *Disciplines in Transformation* had led me to embrace a transformative process that would be a critical engagement among religious, sociological, political, and psychological approaches. Religious symbolization needed to critically engage political theory in order to foster a richer, more viable public life. At the same time, this political symbolism had to deepen the ethical and theological claims at the core of my Christian heritage. I proposed that we lift up the phrase "God's Federal Republic" as "a symbol that can grasp our aspirations as well as stand in judgment on our arrogance." Through it we might identify "elements within both the religious and political sphere which need to be combined in a complex way" reflecting "the critical engagement which is necessary to the life of faith and public action."[3]

Like the body symbol I had analyzed in my dissertation, this symbol contains both rich emotional meaning as well as basic models to frame and guide personal and institutional action. In this project, however, I was not simply analyzing a symbol, as with the body, but writing an apologia for embracing a symbol in which to ground our ethics, worship, and social action.

In proposing this symbolic framework for political ethics, the development of feminist theology was amplifying my earlier engagement with theological expressions of movements for Black liberation. These movements were not merely efforts to fix or reform social life but to reconstitute our fundamental symbolic universe. In our political life it meant a reconstruction of our notions of sovereignty, power, and just order, all of which had deep resonance with theological language about God and God's activity. Changes in both fields of discourse required the process of reciprocal transformation that I had formulated with my colleague Tim Bachmeyer in *Disciplines in Transformation*. Now, however, I was embarked on a substantive task within this formal framework.

---

3. Everett, *God's Federal Republic*, 5.

I knew at the time that this surrender of powerful kingship symbols rooted in "the dark forest of nostalgia" and the adoption of a different symbol, indeed a different map of the terrain altogether, would not be easy. That I would be writing these reflections today in the midst of even more vociferous and dangerous struggles between patriarchal corporate order and democratic, constitutional republicanism was something I didn't anticipate. Intensifying this struggle was the enduring conflict between defenders of a public life founded in agreement among free citizens and proponents of a pseudo-politics confined within the limits of bodily characteristics of race, gender, sex, and ancestry. I can see more clearly how resistance to the reduction of politics to the terms set by our bodies and advocacy for the grace of free citizenship constitute a deep current running throughout my life's work.

The Governing Symbol

I called this complex symbol a "governing symbol," because it orients us to a range of values, action models, and self-understandings that shape our life as persons and participants in wider associations. Governing symbols provide a basic language for talking about how we should live our lives. They empower models of action that move from our personal to our familial, social, and political spheres. Images like body, machine, pyramid, and electromagnetic field, not to mention the computer, have played powerful roles in guiding our action across the many involvements of our lives. They help us to see the world we are in as well as to struggle for a better world to come.

The symbol of "kingdom," I argued, had lost its power and validity in the wake of the republican and democratic revolutions that now inspired our political life. It was grounded in a particular way of ordering life according to our biology and in particular the models of biology from an earlier epoch. It subordinated our image of political order to our models of patriarchal family. Moreover, in its increasing irrelevance to our ethical vision and practical life, it removed the church into a Disneyworld of nostalgia or, even worse, a destructive attack on the political world of republics and constitutional democracy that generations of patriotic citizens had built up over the past two or three centuries.

While the symbol of "republic" has guided much of this political development, the collapse of kingdoms and empires also opened the stage to the horrific onslaught of Fascisms and totalitarianism that had incinerated much of the world as I emerged into it. Images of "people," "community," "body," and even "democracy" had, I argued, significant flaws impairing their capacity to bear the social weight of governance that could replace "kingdom." Even "republic" had to be enlarged with its federal partner, covenant, as well as the values of democratic participation.

Kingdom and Kingship

However, I could not simply set aside the power of kingship symbols. They had had too long a play in our religious and political history. I had to take account of the power and functions they had enjoyed. So I set out to harvest the reasons for the power of this symbol over time and in various cultures from the ancient Near East to the present. While citing the stability of monarchy in Egypt's civilization, I was especially interested in how Israel began with a confederation under Mosaic law before agreeing to a king to "lead them in battle like the other nations" in the time of Samuel.[4] Even this king, they agreed, would be subjected to the covenant of law rather than be the embodiment of it. It was this compromise that introduced the ongoing tension between kingship and a higher order of law that eventually led to the breakdown of kingship as the central governing symbol in the West. Whether it would finally undermine the dominance of kingship in Islamic lands is being fought over bitterly as I write.

As a Christian ethicist and theologian I also had to struggle with the way Jesus of Nazareth became identified as a king who absorbed his other roles as rabbi, priest, savior, healer, and embodied Wisdom of God. In contrast, the tradition of confederal order stretching back to Moses, Elijah, and Samuel could also have been used to understand Jesus and his work. Indeed, I argued, it was always a strain for Matthew and Luke to claim his Davidic descent by putting his birth in Bethlehem rather than Nazareth. In short, there was plenty of room to understand Jesus in terms of other images of governance than kingship.

Drawing on work about medieval kingship by Henry Myers, I pointed out how the Roman empire, which finally absorbed the Christian movement in its own decline, saw in kings merely localized tribal leaders, not the emperor (*imperator*) of its more expansive order. If Jesus was king, he was simply a king among many others in their empire. With the collapse of that empire, kings returned to provide local order. The symbolism of kingship

4. I Sam 8.

and Christ could meld to cement a post-Roman, feudal world still nurtured by the culture of empire.

In spite of their limitations, I pointed out, symbols of kingship enabled people to extend their loyalties from family order to wider domains of government and church life. Kingship symbols provided a model for stability by replicating patriarchal rule in all these arenas. By appealing to the Wisdom of the father and of parents generally, it provided a means to legitimate political order and whatever justice could rule the day.

As kingship absorbed the image of Jesus as the Christ, it also began the process of its own dissolution as the primary governance symbol. Beginning with the baptism of Clovis, King of the Franks, at the end of the fifth century, the attributes of Christ's sovereignty, Wisdom, judgment, and healing were gradually added to kingship. At the same time, inasmuch as individuals were baptized into Christ, they also began to absorb these same virtues of regal dignity and autonomy. By the sixteenth century Christian citizens began to emerge with the attributes of sovereign rulers. The "persona" of Christ, once extended to king and Pope, was being claimed by individuals in the first stirrings of modern democratic self-rule. Though bitterly opposed in church and state, these claims of baptismal self-rule found increasing strength in the sixteenth and seventeenth centuries in northern Europe, England, Scotland, and then in North America. It was one of the chief claims of the Baptist movement that had shaped my early years.

With this evolution, the limits of kingship as a governing symbol emerged. Its roots in patriarchal family, biology, status hierarchy, and personal rule pitted it against the world of contracts, law, individual dignity, conscience, and self-rule that had been nurtured in markets, city councils, and religious movements. The equality of souls embodied in citizenship could not tolerate the survival of monarchy, either in the home or in the emerging public sphere. Patriarchal monarchy rooted governance in biology, while democracy was grounded in the voluntary covenants of people "born again" by grace. Both the liberation of enslaved peoples and feminist claims to full participation in all spheres of life were an inevitable correlate to this religiously rooted democracy.

The Republican Vision

Understanding that kingship was no longer viable, I then turned to explore the republicanism that supplanted it. To do that I returned to the work of Hannah Arendt, whose discussions of public action in *The Human Condition* and *On Revolution* had entered my thought over twenty years earlier. Her elucidation of the difference between private and public realms, between labor and action, necessity and freedom, helped me frame the way Christian theology had been captured by the private sphere of labor and biological necessity. Christian ethics, church practice, and theological reflection had come to focus on the private sphere of family, personality, and interpersonal relations in order to survive a hostile Roman Empire and then to accommodate to a secular sphere of monarchical rule free from theocratic domination. St. Augustine had steered Christian theology into this privatization at the end of the Roman Empire. The rise of a culture of republican and democratic governance challenged us to construct a radically different pattern of interaction between religion and political order.

Arendt's formulation of the meaning of public action helped me reground theological concepts of freedom, grace, and salvation in the language of the public rather than the private realms, even though she herself thought of Christianity almost exclusively as a matter of private ethics and contemplation. Her subsequent employment of these categories to interpret the meaning of the American and French Revolutions of the late eighteenth century grounded these concepts in my own history and the language of democratic republican life. Going beyond her understanding of Christianity, which was unduly restricted by her historical experience, my own effort was a constructively theological one.

What then, have been the enduring marks of republican governance? As with kingship, I set about to trace the lineaments of this tradition, focusing in this case on the values of publicity, stability, equal participation, and persuasion. The Greek *polis* and the Roman *res publica* were sustained not by the life cycle demands of biological necessity, as in the household, but by the work of memory that promised a kind of immortality to rival that of the cosmos. It was a world created by laws, memorable actions, and negotiated agreements. It was not grounded in necessity but in freedom. Restricted as it was to the male heads of households, it nonetheless gave birth to an ideal that would eventually overrun this early vessel.

What it lacked was stability. The delicate balance among participants of equal power inevitably led to the oligarchy of the few, the corruption of wealth, and the rise of the demagogue and tyrant. As I write this, my own republic is threatened by this very dynamic in spite of its 230-year history. The classical solution was a "balanced polity," in which the monarchy, who could lead in battle and unify the people, was balanced by the aristocratic council of elders and the assembly of "the people," who actually carried on the work of the society. This balanced polity later became the "three estates" of late Medieval order and the three branches of government in the modern republican constitution. This struggle for stability through separation of powers began to break down the monolithic view of authority that monarchy had embodied. It also opened up a possible way to envision a pluralism of power within a stable republic. All of this was necessary to provide a space for human freedom.

If individual humans were to be free to interact in a public sphere they had to have a roughly equal access to it. Equality was not merely an economic matter but a constitutional status necessary for participation in the realm of public argument and coordinated common action. Property was not merely a collection of things under one's control but the "props" by which one could enter the drama of public life. Equality without participation, as many state socialisms have shown, does not create human freedom in the republican sense.

A realm of freedom is constituted by a resolution of conflict through persuasion rather than coercion. Persuasion is inherently non-violent. The idea of non-violence itself is not a political concept unless it is connected to the work of persuasion. And persuasion is not possible unless the participants share a roughly common sense of reality grasped by a reason we hold as human beings. This is, of course, an Enlightenment ideal, but it is rooted in a long line of Natural Law thinking going back to the ancient Greeks and Romans. As former Vice-President Albert Gore has pointed out, loss of belief in this reason, this common sense, lies at the core of our cultural and political crisis today.[5]

This republican vision flickered throughout the European Middle Ages in city and church councils, re-emerging in the Renaissance and the many non-state religious movements of the later Reformation. The practices of congregational church order, city councils, and popular assemblies found root in the religious pluralism of the American colonies, leading to the constitutional structure of the separation of powers and the free exercise and non-establishment clauses of the US Constitution's First Amendment.

---

5. Gore, *Assault on Reason*.

Churches and religious institutions generally could participate in the republic only as voluntary associations, not as agencies, ministries, or institutions of government. Governments, in turn, had to be subservient to the political consensus generated by a public in which religious associations played a vital role.

In this complex development the idea and practice of "publicity" became pivotal for my understanding of politics, theology, and, indeed, for the private realm as well. By "publicity" I did not mean advertising flimflam or celebrity worship but the act of participating in a public. Publicity was not only a principle for legitimate governmental action through vigorous participation, persuasion, and artistic freedom, but also a primary psychological motivation in our struggle to claim identity, relationship, and a confirmed existence in the presence of others. It was rapidly becoming central to my understanding of what love itself was about, for in love we reveal ourselves to the other and learn how to confirm what the other person reveals to us. The key concept of publicity resonated not only with my cultural and political heritage but also with the personal work I faced in gaining a public expression for my own experience of a deeply personal love.

This work of publicity in the republican tradition required, however, one more indispensable partner. Historically this had been supplied by the concept and practice of federalism. In my next chapter I set about exploring its heritage and meaning.

Federalism and Covenant

In classical republican thought, public life required a fairly small scale in order to sustain arguments of mutual respect within a common frame of reference. Plato thought about 5,000 citizens would be the limit to the size of a polis. To sustain a larger republican polity, say, for purposes of common defense, the publics would have to be linked in treaty-like relationships. The ancient Hebrew concept of covenant, rooted in treaty relationships, became the religious and political basis for what came to be called federalism. In order to have republican governance people had to live in federations under a common agreement, or constitution. Indeed, the Latin term for covenant, *foedus*, is the root of our English term federalism.

To spell out a normative meaning for this concept I turned to the notion of a "full" covenant that I had begun to elaborate in my land ethics.

The partners of a Biblical covenant are God, the people, and the land. Over time individual persons came to be seen as primary partners in covenantal life. Covenant-making, rather than the biological bonds of kin and tribe, became the essential legitimate bond of public life. This three-fold partnership, amplified by the rise of individual selves as covenant partners, was also becoming central in the OIKOS Project on Work, Family, and Faith, which was emerging in my work at the same time. In its various elaborations, my work on covenant and federalism permeated my research, writing, and teaching for the next twenty years.

As I had done with kingship and republic, I traced the vicissitudes of covenantal and federalist thought through Western history, recounting its submergence in the Roman imperial era and the feudalism of the Middle Ages until its re-emergence in the Renaissance and Reformation. The revival of Biblical theology under the Reformers energized practices of congregational covenant, political covenants, constitutions, and federal governments.

This revival of covenant, however, was also shaped by the rise of individual personhood. People were seizing their status as citizens in governance and contractors in economic life. With this, the full covenant of Biblical thought was in danger of being reduced to self-interested contract. Within this tension I was trying to establish a pattern of enduring relationships that was more than a bundle of limited contracts but other than the biological necessity of kinship, race, and tribe. As I write this, forces of "blood and soil" as well as individual economic greed threaten this constitutional order of covenantal bonds more than ever.

The human struggle for publicity and covenant became the key for my understanding of political theory and theology as well as the theories of personality and society that accompany them. At the same time, the struggle for full publicity, with its exploration of free expression, action, and imagination, often strains at the existing covenantal frameworks underlying the political and legal order. We have only to think of the drive for full publicity of women, of those who had been enslaved and their descendants, of marginalized racial and ethnic groups, and of sexual minorities in altering the constitutional frames and underlying deep covenants of many societies around the world. Simultaneously, as we are experiencing in my own country today, public action and publicity itself require the form of deep covenants to preserve relationships of trust and cooperation in the face of celebrity hucksterism, lies, and misinformation. These twinned and interdependent concepts became the lens for my work in theology and ethics, even as they informed my personal journey in love, work, and family. The symbol of "God's Federal Republic" became, in A. N. Whitehead's language, a "lure" drawing us into a more intense and variegated world of relationships.

A Theory of Covenantal Publicity

Having drawn out a history of public and covenant, I then had to explicate the meaning of this complex notion of covenantal publicity. First, I had to clarify what I meant by "public" and "publicity." I modified the characteristics of republican thinking to emphasize the values of participation, commonality, persuasion, and worldliness. To these I added the dynamics of emancipation, legitimation, and pluralism. I see now that this list was unnecessarily awkward. It is more straightforward to list the four characteristics of covenantal publicity as (1) participation, resting on the dynamic of emancipation, (2) commonality and persuasion as the ground of legitimation, (3) pluralism, and (4) worldliness.

Underlying participation is the need for some rough equality of power. However, equality is not the primary value. It exists in order to facilitate participation. The seeming "equality" of individuals under various forms of Communism betrayed the very essence of public life at this point. Equality, like property, exists to make it possible to engage in the drama of public life. At this point I was seeking to press beyond the "possessive individualism" (C. B. Macpherson's term) of liberal economics to a concept of "public personality." Here I can see, from my vantage point years later, an intellectual expression of my own life's struggle to move from a self-definition grounded in my economically privileged youth to a more public life as a teacher and writer.

In public participation we emancipate ourselves from the limits of private existence, whether in free households or various forms of coerced privation and slavery. Drawing on Hannah Arendt's theory of action and Jürgen Habermas's theory of communication, I emphasized our need and capacity to profess our inner needs, interests, and claims. In the interaction of these multiple professions we develop a sense of a public confirmation of our identity and our place in the larger world. What I did not emphasize enough at the time was the correlative task of confirming, correcting, and transforming the professions of others in the public realm. This task is made even more difficult when we retreat to our own silos of self-confirmation, launching missiles of contempt and deception across the empty public square.

To engage in this activity of profession and confirmation we need enough cultural commonality to make the work of language, argument, and persuasion possible. The clash of private interests can be mediated in the public, but the clash of worldviews without any common benchmark of adjudication—whether scientific, cultural, or religious—spells the death of the public and the rise of the authoritarian and the demagogue. Today, in 2021, the search for commonality amidst demagoguery is even more pressing than when I wrote this in 1985.

Without substantial commonality the work of persuasion becomes impossible. Without common standards of reason and truth, violence invades the public realm. Strength replaces legitimate authority as the basis of governance. The work of persuasion also involves symbolic speech, art, drama, and ritual. Persuasion has to engage the roots of motivation as well as of cognition. Even in this work of argument and persuasion we are constantly testing and re-working the fundamental covenants that bind us together as a public. Reason itself has a covenantal character to it, just as the work of scientists occurs in a covenant about testing, replication, verification, and public inspection. But this is a far cry from the kind of solipsism that passes for critical thinking today, in which each person affirms the truth or falsehood of the other without being constrained by a common reason for adjudicating differences.

In a covenantal public the work of legitimation is rooted in the complex web of fundamental agreements worked out over time and tested by experience. Historically grounded covenantal bonds crystallize in constitutions that need to be continually adjusted in changing circumstances. Legitimacy rests not in the biological fixities of sex and physiognomy but in the patient work of persuasive reason.

Establishing the commonality underlying public life is one of the traditional functions of religion. In order to do this, it has to give up the struggle for power, which would only subject it to the argumentation and conflict of the public sphere. However, it cannot simply remove its claims into some other world, whether private or supernatural. Here my deep roots in the American Constitutional traditions of "non-establishment" and "free exercise" remained central for me, even as I gave them a particular grounding within the broader federal-republican tradition. This was not only a public claim I was making. It was also a fundamental rationale for the cultural work that occupied my life, often somewhat distant to the immediate claims of politics itself.

The work of persuasion and covenant presumes a pluralism of interests, worldviews, and needs. Moreover, the work of reasonable persuasion requires debate among minds limited by our finitude, intelligence, and understanding, not to mention the passions of particular loves and fears. We each need to enlarge as well as limit each other. This is the classic understanding of conciliar government, in which wisdom can only be sought among a group of diverse minds.

As groups, institutions, and even nation states arise out of intense webs of mutually-confirmed loyalties, we once again need to turn to covenantal arrangements among these wider collectives, both to limit their reach and also to combine their energies for common purposes. Eventually this leads us to the challenge of forming some sort of world federalism. The United Nations, rooted in the concept of national sovereignties, constitutes the present form of this search, but also contains an intrinsic limitation. The myth of national sovereignty strictly limits how much covenantal mutuality can be attained. As I write this, it is being sorely tested by nationalisms of all kinds, threatening our capacity to erect forms of governance capable of dealing with the threat of global ecological catastrophe.

While I could not envision this threat adequately at the time, I was led by Hannah Arendt's work to site the need for "worldliness." I would not use this term today. Perhaps "ecology" or "material grounding" get at the idea. What I wanted to do was include the land, the earth on which we live, as critical for a public. What was starting to emerge in my thought, as it was for many others, was the need for attention to an underlying ecological system as necessary for a public. No public can survive if it despoils its ecological context. Here I was being informed by my work on land ethics. The air we breathe, the water we drink, the soil, animals, and the biological life we depend on for our existence have to have a voice in the public. The idea of "worldliness" was simply a marker for this idea.

We are now experiencing the outer limits of what the earth can sustain in relation to the way humans are organizing their lives politically and economically. The struggle for an adequate form of world federalism resting in a new covenant about our relation to the earth is its political expression.[6]

---

6. See Bosselman and Engel, *Earth Charter*, and many related publications about this leading effort to articulate such a vision.

How all the parties to this covenanted republic, especially the land and God, can be represented in the public argument remains unclear and very contested. What was clear to me was that to have them not represented at all was perilous in any struggle toward the vision of God's Federal Republic.

Covenantal publicity was thus a very rich term that sought to hold together the work of building and acting in publics with the work of entering into covenants and federal relationships that both sustain and relate these publics to one another and, finally, to earth itself and the history in which it lives. Each side of this term constantly invokes and shapes the other. In the concept of covenantal publicity lay the theoretical components that later undergirded my intense interest in promoting reconciling conversations as the key to restorative justice. Moreover, this was not merely a secular political concept, but also a way of envisioning the work of the Spirit enlivening the ecclesia where Christ presides. My later work in the church and my communities has involved bringing people from sexual and racial minorities into the full public realm. I see now more clearly how it is rooted in the political and theological reconstruction worked out in *God's Federal Republic*.

A Psychological Theory: The Performer Self

Having laid down the fundaments of this composite vision, I then sketched the perspective on psychology that fits this construction of covenantal publicity. Here I was once again following the trilateral methodological commitments I had made in my earlier work. While I worked these issues out more fully in *Blessed Be the Bond*, which I will discuss shortly, in this context I simply wanted to adumbrate the psychological dynamics of profession and confirmation. While still deeply indebted to the conflict psychologies of Freudians and Jungians, I turned here to the humanist fulfillment schools, stressing that "the self is led by a longing for publicity." This again was an emphasis borne out of my own struggle for a fuller emotional life grounded in my own inner constitution.

This struggle for more adequate self-expression and confirmation leads us to ever wider arenas of publicity, starting with the "little theaters" of the home and moving to schools, churches, associations, political parties, and more general publics. In this complex activity of profession and confirmation we seek to establish stable bonds of mutual understanding. We seek covenantal structures that recognize our emancipatory struggle for profession but also our need for stable public worlds of confirmation. Thus, the self is not only *homo publicans* (public-seeking human) but also *homo foedans* (covenantal human), to use the Latin terms I coined to go beyond *homo sapiens, homo faber* (human maker) and the rest.

In spelling out the nature of this personal work of covenant-making I once again turned to the full list of covenant partners: self, people, land, and God. In describing the divine partner I attended briefly to the problem of symbolizing God as parent, partner, creator and governor. The way that land, indeed a particular configuration of land and water, shapes our deepest self-understandings became a theme later in my work on the "oikos" of work, family, and faith. What it is to claim membership among a people became critical in my later work on religion and federalism. I realize now, with the acute contention over what "the people" means in American law and culture, that I have never fully worked out this dimension of covenantal thought adequately. With my own personal journey at the time into deeper personhood, my main focus at this point was to develop the psychology of the self that seeks wider and wider publics of self-definition and expression. I called this type of personality a "performer self."

In this context I took the time to discuss the problem of narcissism. The self-regarding energies of narcissism are indispensable for the initial act of profession into an unknown public. However, a narcissistic personality is unable to enter into the wider process of confirmation entailed in stable covenants and repeated self-correction. Instead of seeing someone engaged in the work of publicity in a viable public, we have the celebrity who seeks only a passive, admiring audience. As I said at the time, "The narcissistic personality oscillates wildly between feverish playing to the grandstand and enormous self-doubt."[7] The narcissistic personality either ends up destroying the public and private realms around himself or herself (what I came to call "the black hole effect") or retreating into phantasmal self-isolation. The proper publicity of the citizen is corrupted into the narcissism of the celebrity who must either dominate the public world or reduce it to the mirror halls of self-adulation.

While I saw this danger at the heart of a self that is engaged in public life, I could not imagine at the time that such a personality would take over the Presidency of the United States. It is both a symptom of the critical decay of our public realm as well as a further threat to its recovery. At the time, I could only point at the importance of maintaining the many and

---

7. Everett, *God's Federal Republic*, 152.

diverse publics to contain the publically destructive narcissistic personality until it and the audience sustaining it burns out like a supernova explosion.

The vision of a covenantal public and the kind of personality that emerges in it led me to the final and ultimate grounding of such a vision. Just as narcissism constituted a kind of necessary sin for the self, and the breaking of covenants and federations as the primary form of alienation, so this federal republican vision led me to its theological ground.

Theological Transformations

God's Federal Republic sought to reconstruct theological language under the impact of the change in the structure and language of governance from monarchy to republics. It was therefore important for me to spell out some key implications of this theological reconstruction for political ethics and ecclesiology.

The symbol "God's Federal Republic" sought to carry forth major values embedded in the biblical governance themes of covenant and confederation, while also expanding the hard-won republican, democratic, and constitutional values that were fed by notions of baptismal citizenship, public preaching, and ecclesial autonomy. This symbol was engaged enough in republican culture to legitimate its aspirations. At the same time, it was distant enough from our actual limited attainments to be a source of judgment as well as hope. Here, I can only list the major points I tried to illuminate at the time. Each was only a proposal for further development, only some of which I have been able to explore in subsequent work.

First, I emphasized how theological language itself is a performative act of publicity, one rooted most clearly in public worship and prophetic action. This emphasis has continued and deepened in my work on ethics and worship, the liturgical grounding of ecological and restorative justice, and my subsequent poetry, hymnody, and liturgy. Having laid down this foundational perspective, I proceeded to some of the traditional categories of theology.

Salvation, I argued, can be seen as the struggle for ever-fuller covenantal publicity. We set aside the lies, secrecy, fear, and darkness that hide us from ourselves and each other in order to emerge into a public of truth, openness, and trust. We are able to act in full profession as well as honest confirmation. The resurrection of the body, I pointed out, can be understood as a way to say that action, which is inextricable from our unique bodies, is sustained in its perfection in salvation. From the standpoint of covenantal publicity, salvation requires some sort of "body," a claim that harked back to my dissertation, in which I tried to understand why "body thinking" was so pervasive in social thought and theology. However, this was a new dimension in my reflection on this powerful metaphor.

I think now it would have been interesting to explore the ways visions of heaven need to be seen in their connection to actual political visions of perfected action. Rather than critique them for their other-worldliness, we might see these visions as ways of imagining the perfection of covenantal publicity. Heavenly visions, songs, and theologies have accompanied the whole history of the American republic and continue in the popular religion of many Americans. The work of this envisioning goes far beyond nations. It is an indispensable work of the church as the seed of perfected covenantal publicity in the light of God's ultimate federal republic.

The key activities of the church—baptism, eucharist, confession, and preaching—can all be understood as ways to symbolize and advance the fuller life of covenantal publicity grounded in God. I had already lifted up the importance of baptismal practices in linking Christ's kingship to earthly kings and then later to citizens. Eucharist, as I was to develop it much more fully in my work on roundtable worship, could be seen as an ancient symposium of conversation governed by the spirit of Christ's presidency rather than being confined to understanding it as commemoration of a sacrificial Passover. Confession, even within the confidential priest-parishioner context, could be understood as the first step in publicizing the inner self. Preaching, of course, is a quintessentially public act and a defining mark of the Christian ecclesia, at least in the broad tradition of the Western church. It is also central to the worship practices of Judaism and Islam. All of these acts are "sacramental," in the sense of taking a worldly, public action and using it to engage participants in the work of entering into wider publics and covenants grounded in God. Here, the church emerges as a little theater of a more perfect publicity within its environing societies. In my later work on religion and federalism, this core ecclesiological concept of the church as a nucleus of publicity became a key descriptive as well as prescriptive concept.

If this is the meaning of salvation, then sin is exclusion from fuller publicity and covenanted relationship. Evil is the very structure of darkness, alienation, and silence that hinders this salvation. This is an obvious reconstruction of Augustine's theory of sin as a form of privation, but here it is privation from the perfect public of God's self-revelation and our response. As in many theological matters throughout my life, Augustine was once again both foil and foe in my articulation of a different path.

The understanding of God at the center of this theological perspective points us beyond the limits of our feeble hopes and our shallow achievements. From the standpoint of the symbol of "God's Federal Republic," God is Covenanter, Publisher and President. Our own work of covenant-making is grounded in the ultimate reality that the universe is a covenantal action of God. Here I was reaching all the way back to my study of Karl Barth as well as to the biblical record itself.

With the terminology of "publisher" and "president," I was drawing on the process theology arising from the adoption of Alfred North Whitehead's philosophy as the framework for a philosophical theology. God's creative and redemptive activity is a work of more expansive publication of our lives and, indeed, of the life of God. Freed from fear and bound in love we have the courage to publish our own existence before others. This is the liberating moment of the divine-human engagement. Drawing further from Whitehead, I construed God as President of the public in which we move further into this covenanted republic. God is best understood as presiding within this realm of full publicity. This imagery, of course, beckons us to re-think questions of God's power, omniscience, and responsibility for evil. One way to approach this was to understand God as the "Logos"—the logic—of the public discourse of this fully realized covenantal republic.

With the introduction of the idea of the Logos, I turned to images of Jesus as the Christ, who is understood here as ecclesial president. This was, in a sense, a very Catholic move, informed by my years of immersion in Catholic thought and practice. It is in the public assembly that we recognize Jesus as the Christ. There is no Christ aside from the public in which he presides. This view was far removed from the Jesus-in-the-garden (alone!) that blew softly in my ears as a child. Jesus engaged in a ministry that liberated marginalized, silenced people into a wider public where God presides. Jesus exercised the work of publisher in his healing, listening, teaching and praying. His presidency emerged in his discourse and his own offering of himself in a life of persuasion over against the coercive, murderous forces of ordinary people. He continues to preside "in the Spirit" in this ongoing assembly where the works of healing, listening, confession, baptismal profession, and preaching continue to liberate people into a more expansive covenantal publicity.

Thus we come to the Holy Spirit, which obviously plays a larger role in this theological reconstruction than it has often played in Christian theology. In a patriarchal era it was relegated to being the bond between the Father and the Son. Like a mediating mother, it (or she) hovered in the shadows of theology. In this theological reconstruction, the Holy Spirit, as at Pentecost, continues as the source of the language-transcending conversation of the ecclesia. The role of the church's leadership is to preside in this conversation and to care for this ongoing work of covenantal publicity. Their presidency, however, is always a kind of vice-presidency that tries to stand in for the Spirit of Christ. This construct became the core of my ecclesiology, something that I worked out methodically in subsequent books, liturgies, and songs.

A Retrospective Assessment

This book-length argument constituted a theological program more than a full exposition. Though steeped in German theology, I did not proceed to a multi-volume exposition of this perspective in a systematic way. Partly, this was because building such an audacious cathedral was beyond my allocated energy or years. More significant, perhaps, is that my commitment to this ongoing, ever-expanding conversation of God's public meant that no seemingly complete systematic statement should even be attempted.

In any event, I look back on it now as the hinge point in my intellectual development, since it spoke from the core of my theological and cultural heritage but also led me in a particular way into uncharted territory, only some of which I have been able to map in subsequent years. It took me from the methodological efforts of assembling the key partners in my ongoing discussion toward the more substantive commitments of the next years. Most of my subsequent work rode on the rails laid down here. The desperate struggles my country and my church find themselves in today only intensify its call for a theology more critically engaged with our political culture.

Theologically, I can see more clearly how my reconstruction owed as much to a renewed eschatology as it did to a new cosmology or doctrine of creation. Public action, being always a movement into the freedom of the future, has to be grounded in a vision of the new creation God is creating if it is not to fall back into nostalgia or resentful tribal longing for a lost past. In grasping the connection of this eschatological vision to public life, I believe even more strongly that the patriarchal symbols of the monarchical traditions in our Christian liturgies have served to legitimate the current resurgence of patriarchal politics and culture. At the same time, the persistence of medieval nostalgia in our symbols undergirds reactionary politics that fail to address the economic injustice and ecological disaster arising in extreme climate change. Finally, our inability to generate a plausible framework for bonding personal spirituality with political action undermines the vitality of both public and private life.

Awareness of this intricate connection between the personal, private, and public informed my exploration of the private world in a companion volume. Treatments of post-patriarchal religion and of ecological ethics emerged later in other formats.

Blessed Be the Bond

In the mid-1970s I began teaching a course on marriage and family with some of my colleagues at St. Francis Seminary. These included Rev. Kenneth Smits OFM Cap., a teacher of liturgical theology, Rev. Andrew Nelson, an ethicist, Rev. Kenneth Metz, in pastoral care, and others. This initiative continued and expanded the interdisciplinary work I had introduced into the curriculum earlier. While women were beginning to find a way into the faculty and student body, my immediate milieu for this task was the school's core of Roman Catholic priests and priesthood students.

In my personal crises at the end of that decade, I needed to grapple with renewed intensity with the questions at the heart of this course. This may seem to some to be a strange context for grappling with the many dimensions of divorce and remarriage, but I found that my Catholic colleagues had far less moralistic and rigid sensibilities in confronting these problems than many of my Protestant clergy friends. Moreover, they approached these personal and interpersonal issues with a much greater sense of their theological depth and complexity. Perhaps because of the centrality of confession and absolution in their religious practice, they were more aware that we live by constantly renewed grace than were many of my Protestant friends, who had reduced their faith life to ethics and moral striving.

With this background I was both highly motivated and supported in trying to make sense of my own experience of the fracturing of my marital and family bonds as well as their reconstruction on new bases. The sociological and psychological literature on these matters was and remains enormous. However, theological literature that took into account both my experience and an interdisciplinary approach to reflection on it was meager indeed. In the wake of this overwhelming experience I was challenged to draw on my interdisciplinary method in order to provide guidance for a broader public and at the same time explicate the substantive commitments that had been forged in my own experience. As I did this, I was very conscious of the way this effort was a companion to *God's Federal Republic*, both in time and in thought.

As with *God's Federal Republic*, I was approaching this task as one of interpreting, re-ordering, and reconstructing central symbols and models of theological thought and practice. In particular, I had to emphasize the distinction between a symbol and a metaphor. Many of the things that we say about marriage—that it is a sacrament, a divinely authored institution, and the like— confuse these two functions of words. I had experienced the difference between saying marriage is a symbol of God's fidelity, for example, and saying that it is a metaphor for God's fidelity. I had experienced more deeply that when we use marriage as a symbol, we try to make sure that marriage reflects all the attributes of God's fidelity that we have declared elsewhere in our faith. Marriage becomes an instrument for expressing faith. In employing marriage as a metaphor, we use some characteristic we have experienced in marriage or family to try to express what God's faithfulness is like. Marriage as metaphor is a source of religious understanding but not an instrument of an understanding gained elsewhere in religious life. In my own life I had moved from trying to make my marriage a theological symbol to exploring my marital experience for metaphors for the divine-human encounter.

Secondly, I emphasized, again from my experience, that various models of relationships can be attached to the same general theological symbol for marriage. Calling it a "sacrament" or a "covenant" can actually convey very different models for our relationships in particular historical, cultural, or societal contexts. I, myself, had moved in this time of transition from one model of relationship to another as well as from one cluster of theological symbols to another. In this book I laid out this framework and this reconstructed understanding by beginning with the sociological context and psychological patterns underlying my own experience and the broader social history in which I was immersed. I then proceeded to the theological task of understanding this experience and guiding my new life.

Commitments and Convictions

The Subjects of Marriage

I began by asking what human state or relationship is being called a sacrament, covenant, vocation, or a communion. What reality (in Roman Catholic theology, what *res*), is actually experiencing "marriage" in the act of union or "divorce" in the shattering of a marital bond? From my experience and study, it had become obvious that the "subject" of marriage had shifted due to deep sociological changes. What had been one fused subject had differentiated over the centuries. The original subject of marriage was actually four subjects that were fused together: the person, the couple, the family, and the household. I came to call this constellation of subjects the "oikos," after the ancient Greek name for household. This was the nub of what became the OIKOS Project on Work, Family, and Faith.

The original subject of the church's focus was the procreative couple, which was inseparable from the family and household they generated. Over time, this original oikos had differentiated. Women could now be persons without being spouses or daughters. Because of the proliferation of increasingly specialized occupations in the industrial revolution, each person could create his or her own household, with or without children. With this differentiation each person accrued increasing autonomy and citizenship, whether in the economy, the polity, or the home.

It was this differentiation of the oikos that required a theological reconstruction in terms of self-understanding as well as of the relation of the church to family, society, and the state. It was a differentiation that I had experienced in my own life. I had entered marriage as a bond of parental care and control rather than as a conjugal union of equal mates. The expectations of marriage and the meaning of personhood had shifted, seemingly suddenly, under my feet. And I was not alone, as the divorce statistics showed. Dedication to parental stability had yielded to the primacy of the skills of autonomy, communication, and negotiation. The marriage I had entered as a social duty could no longer be sustained. Its failure and the discovery of new possibilities now required a profound renovation of my psychological foundations as well as my theological outlook.

At the same time, my long experience in educating students for the Roman Catholic priesthood had deepened my understanding of the Church's original suspicions of marriage and family as well as of the markedly different relationships between church and family order that were possible within a Christian framework. The priesthood, which had been separated from marriage in the late Middle Ages in order to preserve the Church's autonomy, was now facing a world in which every marriage was being separated from work, wider family, and political institutions. I sketched out this shift in an address in Milwaukee to the Catholic Theological Society of America in 1978, published as "Between Augustine and Hildebrand: A Critical Response to Human Sexuality."

For both myself and my friends in the Catholic priesthood, history and cultural context required a more nuanced approach to the theological meaning of marriage and family and their relation to the society around them. It was simply impossible to assume a univocal relationship among theological symbols, personal psychology, family order, church practice, and patterns of marital relationships. Political reaction and resistance to these long developments have only intensified since I wrote this book, a symptom of the deep threat they pose to traditional patriarchal orders.

The Theological Symbols

Out of the basket of theological symbols that have been attached to marriage and family I chose four that seemed paramount in history and in my experience: sacrament, covenant, vocation, and communion. Sacrament focuses us on the deep symbolic, ritual life of the church. While there have been numerous sacramental theories, they generally emphasize the way in which our natural life and its elements (bread, wine, water, earth, and sex) can be media of divine power and purpose. "Nature" and "grace" can be intermingled in ways that transform the earthly into the heavenly. Because, however, all these earthly things are finite and fragile, they constantly fail in this self-transcending task, so that an elaborate practice of providing for confession, forgiveness, and renewal needs to sustain these practices of sacramental grace.

The concept of vocation, rooted in the biblical notion of God's calling of Israel, originally implied for Christians only the calling to the higher life of holiness, something the early church had difficulty associating with the married life, with its absorption in children, household, and familial duties, not to mention sex. Out of this came the Medieval church's division of Christian life into those who were called (monks first, then priests) and the laity (Christians engaged in non-monastic or non-priestly life). It was only in the Reformation and later times, with the further differentiation of the oikos into a multiplicity of occupations, that marriage could emerge as a vocation along with the other major full-time activities of life. Once marriage could become a choice, it could take on more aspects of the kind of intentionality associated with monastery and priesthood.

Covenant, rooted in biblical thought and practice, especially in Israel's memory, emphasizes the way our relationship with God is a promissory relationship binding us to a common purpose. In biblical times its primary form was a "suzerainty" covenant between a superior lord and a vassal. This, as many scholars pointed out, was the primary form used to talk of God's relationship with Israel. Sometimes, however, covenants between equals emerged, as with David and Jonathan, but these did not fare well as models for divine-human relationship. It was only much later, in the Reformation era, that covenant came to be applied to marriage, which the Reformers had separated from its sacramental moorings. Protestant covenantal theories of marriage then had to struggle with the tensions between the patriarchal model of a suzerainty covenant over against the friendship of a covenant between equals.

Like sacrament, covenant provided a form for the experience of broken promises, sin, forgiveness, and renewed relationship. Ordinary human promises are constantly being broken and often being renewed. However, the unbreakable covenant between Yahweh and Israel, reinforced in Christian theology with its idea of the new or "fresh" covenant in Christ, emphasized the unbroken forgiveness of God even as it could be used to reinforce the unbreakable character of the marriage bond.

While the idea of communion, even erotic communion, and its theological implications stretches back to the Bible's Song of Songs, marriage as communion that links us to God awaited much later development, first in Romantic literature and then in theology. Here, the kind of mutual love that reflects the love ethic of John's Gospel and the Letters of John links the life of the couple to the divine life. Marital love, detached from the historic legal and economic inequality between men and women, could be used to talk about the mystical union of persons with God. Marital love was a primary symbol of the divine communion with the world. In this, it could find links to the doctrine of the Trinity, with its mysterious love among the "persons" in the Godhead.

I explored these four symbols in considerable detail in this book and elsewhere. These constituted the four theological partners in the interchange between social subjects, theology, and the three basic models of relationship.

Models of Relationship

In order to fill out the way these theological symbols interacted with the four subjects of marriage and family, I needed to rework the societal models in *Disciplines in Transformation* to lift up three models of relationships that seemed to predominate in marriage and family over the centuries: hierarchical, organic, and egalitarian. While they did not fit exactly the broader societal patterns I identified in *Disciplines*, they seemed to arise more readily out of history and my own experience.

Hierarchical relationships invoke the traditional image of a pyramid of power and authority. This relational model has attributed power and authority, given by nature and by God, to the father of the family. In its strictest form women are always under the control of a male family member, whether it is the father, the brother, or the husband. In its softer form it produces a relationship of paternal care and loving control. To accommodate this version I sometimes called this a subordinationist model.

The organic model is often overlooked, but I have found it widespread in situations where the spouses are immersed in a common task that orders their daily life. The actions of command fall into the background as the husband and wife carry out the duties necessitated by household enterprise and family. The family farm is the most obvious example of this context. It was exemplified in the words of a farm couple Sylvia and I interviewed in connection with the OIKOS Project. The wife firmly declared to us: "I believe the man should be the head of the household, so I let him make the big decisions."

The egalitarian model has emerged to cultural dominance in advanced industrial societies, where each spouse has an independent economic power within a democratic civil and legal order. This is the context within which emotional intimacy and sophisticated communication are necessary to the survival and functioning of the marriage. The marriage becomes more fragile but its rewards for personal happiness become greater. As the bonds of children, work, and community fall away, the two individuals in the marriage have to sustain their common world out of their own psychological resources. Raised in the cultural umbrella of the first two models, like many of my generation, I had to find my way in a world dominated by the third.

COMMITMENTS AND CONVICTIONS

The Harvest, the Winnowing, and the Bread

To map the interplay of sociological subjects, theological symbols and relational models, I returned to use of a grid-work like those in *Disciplines in Transformation*. As I have developed my woodworking in these later years, I can see these "Everettian grids," as one reviewer called them, as a kind of cabinetry that speaks to a deep need for ordering the complexities of experience, just as I do with the many pieces of wood that go to make up a chest of drawers.

With this grid I could at least point to the many permutations of these approaches to marriage and family over the centuries. I could identify some strong affinities among them as well as get a more graphic sense of the changes that had occurred in recent centuries as well as in my own life. The steady movement from hierarchical and organic models to egalitarian patterns was obvious. The shift from traditional sacramental, covenantal, and vocational models to patterns of communion rose to the surface for greater exploration. The fragility and deep challenges of an increasingly fragmented oikos led me into the work that found expression in the OIKOS Project arising from the constructive work in *Blessed Be the Bond* and *God's Federal Republic*.

Issues and Outcomes

In claiming for marriage the communion symbol and a more egalitarian model of relationship I came to stress more strongly that marriage and family are first of all natural parts of ordinary human life. We must first come to them in their sheer dynamic naturalness. They are first of all born of our emotions, intuition, and innate constitutions before they can become an ethical project or a theological symbol. In terms of my own loyalties, marital covenant could not be sustained without marital communion.

In starting with this natural base I could then gain a different sense of the relation of nature and grace. My Protestant, largely Calvinist, upbringing had emphasized the radical otherness of grace as a kind of legal forgiveness that changed my status but not my actual life, other than to leave a residue of anxious wondering about my inevitably broken self. Catholic understanding, flowing from Thomas Aquinas, had emphasized ways that grace could be a divine power "perfecting" nature, beginning with the actual life I was living. I now could see a more complex interweaving of these two dimensions as I worked at my own reconstruction and new relationships with persons and institutions around me. In Methodist traditions flowing from John Wesley, this "perfecting grace" became a much more tangible guide to my spiritual experience.

Even as I was forced to take a more distanced, "professional" stance toward church, public institutions, and even my parental tasks, I was also claiming a new and different connection to them that would have to be worked out in coming decades. They included seeing parenthood as a more public covenant that requires a complex system of support among many public institutions. I spent some time in the 1980s working out the implications of a parental covenant in situations of divorce or marital separation, trying to anchor in law the stability of parenthood for both parents in spite of the weaknesses of the marital bond. This effort included working with a custody reform group in Wisconsin as well as writing an article, "Shared Parenthood in Divorce: The Parental Covenant and Custody Law," in the *Journal of Law and Religion*. In this area, at least, the states have generally pursued legal and judicial policies that focus on strengthening parental bonds even as they allow spouses to end their marriages when they no longer offer a chance for bonds of communion to survive.

Though egalitarian marriage is indeed more fragile, the skills of communication and empathy that it requires are in greater demand in the complex publics emerging in a high-technology era. As marriages of communion became more prevalent they needed new forms of stability. To respond to this need, some of the structures of work would have to be reshaped by conceiving of couples as having a joint vocation in the world. Rather than trying to simply be a symbol of sacramental fidelity, couples might find ways of bringing unique gifts from their marriage to the church and their communities. What I could only see later was that the autonomy of persons underlying communion marriages would begin to foster marital relationships among persons with different sexual orientations and gender identities, challenging churches to come to terms with the gifts they might bring to the communities in which they live. All of these strands would take many years to develop in my own thought and life, stretching to this day later in retirement.

Recent political events have sharpened the way in which the communication and collaborative skills that women have had to develop to function in hierarchical, subordinationist models have not only been transferred to egalitarian marriages but are reshaping work and politics. It is now men who are having real difficulty adapting to the demands of work and political life in a world of communication, where brain power and cybernetics replaces brawn and muscle. This is the main connection between the rise of egalitarian marriage and truly democratic, republican governance.

Even as my family's farm slipped out of production and my father's possession, images of harvest and winnowing guided my poetic mind as I tried to make sense of these changes and proceed to make whatever new bread would be possible in the next phase of my life. My graduate school friend Jim Fowler had just brought out his important study *Stages of Faith*. Along with Daniel Levinson's *Seasons of a Man's Life*, these books could help me understand additional ways I was in a transition to a fundamentally new way of living and understanding my life.

In particular I came to a deeper awareness of how faith was not merely a set of beliefs or worldviews, but a set of trustworthy relationships. The failure of marital relationship in my own life and the new relationships that were emerging had constituted a deep crisis in my theology and spirituality. In their re-forging I was gaining a transformed faith as well as theology. This view of faith as trustworthy relationship flowed into the OIKOS Project as well as into my approach to ethics and worship in my later years.

As I was completing these manuscripts and inaugurating the OIKOS Project I received an invitation in 1985 to join the faculty at the Candler School of Theology at Emory University. Going to Atlanta brought me back to the southern Appalachians, but to an unfamiliar city at the heart of the Civil Rights struggle as well as a burgeoning new Southern economy and society. In addition, it gave me the opportunity to work with some old friends like Jon Gunnemann, with whom I ended up teaching courses on economic ethics and the introduction to Christian ethics. It offered an opportunity to develop my professional agenda and add to it in the form of administering their professional doctoral programs. My basket was, indeed, overflowing.

IV

Practices

The OIKOS Project on Work, Family and Faith

THE OIKOS PROJECT SYNTHESIZED the public and private perspectives of *God's Federal Republic* and *Blessed Be the Bond* into an adult education program as well as a teaching and research agenda that lasted into the late 1990s. Sylvia joined me in both the public presentations and some of the research in addition to her own work in the arts and in humanities administration.

    The OIKOS Project lay at the heart of my effort to conceptualize what was happening in my own work and family life as well as in the society around me. As I thought about a way to grasp these changes and transformations, I turned to a word and concept not found in English but in ancient Greek—*oikos*. The ancient Greek word *oikos* embraced not only the dwelling but the family and household living in it, much as the ancient Hebrew *bayith* (or *beth*) meant household. In most of these ancient agrarian cultures the "house," as in "the house of Israel," included the whole patrimonial legacy of the "name." With this name, and here I was picking up what Denis Fustel de Coulanges had laid out in *The Ancient City*, came the rituals and beliefs that legitimated this life at the ancestral hearth. The land supporting this house economically and physically was included in this expansive notion of "oikos."

I called this the "fused" oikos in which self, family, household, and land were one person in the drama of life and history. English has no comparable word to convey the inherent connection among these often disconnected components of our life. "Oikos," with its cognates in "economics," "ecology," and "ecumenics," met this need. This fused oikos had gradually differentiated over the centuries into a pattern in the late industrial world where persons, work, family, household, faith, and the land were increasingly independent of each other. One could be a person without being married, a productive worker without being a member of a household in the enterprise, a worshipper without being a family member in that worshipping association, and so on.

It was in this ever-differentiating oikos that a public sphere arose in which people could act increasingly as autonomous persons, whether they were men or women, married or unmarried, and, in our time, gay, straight, or non-binary. To dramatize this complex development, I began to move around colorful cutout cardboard figures with magnetic strips on their backs on a metal whiteboard. When this long cultural development was laid out on the whiteboard, people could even sense the stresses and strains they were experiencing trying to hold their oikos together in this fragmented situation as the figures were moved around to reflect the differentiation and reconfigurations of their oikos.

Underlying this presentation was the belief that each component of the original fused oikos is crucial to our human well-being. Our life task, in a world that does not automatically combine them for us, is to find a way to hold them together that honors our commitments to autonomy, love, and sustainability, among other values. We do this by uncovering and honoring our "governing oikos image," the inner emotional sense of how these components should be rightly ordered. This struggle for a right ordering of our trustworthy relationships is the primary form through which we try to express what it is to be faithful in life.

Using this perspective, I explored how vocation and calling, once anchored in the life of the Hebrew people, had become individualized in the Christian conception of the saint and monk. The core of this idea had come to me through the teaching of James Luther Adams and the seminal article by Karl Holl on the history of the concept of calling.[1] As Max Weber had pointed out in *The Protestant Ethic and the Spirit of Capitalism*, the individualized Christian ideal in turn had led to the Protestant concept of

---

1. Holl, "Beruf."

an individual's life-long commitment to an occupation. This was the core of the work culture we had inherited and which has become increasingly secularized as it unraveled into the shriveled concept of the job or gig.

Simultaneously, covenant, in becoming individualized in the theology of personal salvation and a personal covenant with Christ, had lost its capacity to draw us into wider webs of relationship, whether in work, community, or public life. Reduced to simple contract, based on the self-interest of the individuals involved, it served the interests of a fissiparous capitalism rather than the bonds of community, association, and nation. The life task addressed by the OIKOS Project was how to preserve some of the individualized and public values of personhood and voluntary association while honoring our deep human need for connection, relationship, and a sense of transcendent grounding for our lives, both individually and in various communities and publics.

In the OIKOS Project I found a way to manipulate vivid images as a method in my thinking and teaching. There was a certain degree of performance art here as well, as I moved the figures representing various components around on the whiteboard. In my teaching and writing I used it to explicate the meaning of covenant, vocation, stewardship, church administration, and marriage and family issues. It also guided my research in family studies, law, ecclesiology, economic ethics, and ecology. From 1984 to 1995 Sylvia and I used this framework to lead almost a hundred workshops in churches, schools, and corporate environments.

After we had resettled to Atlanta, Sylvia and I conducted a sociological survey of couples who work together to find out how they put their own oikos together. Our research emerged as "Couples at Work: A Study of Patterns of Work, Family, and Faith" in a volume of essays edited by my friend and colleague Nancy Ammerman and sociologist Wade Clark Roof. This provided a way for us to envision our own suitable vocational pattern as we explored how different work patterns were allied with different patterns of marriage and family relationships as well as faith orientations. It was quite clear, for instance, that the tighter or more fused oikos patterns had a strong affinity with hierarchical marital relationships. Relationships in which the oikos was more open or even fragmented led to marital patterns of equality and communion. Both of these implied differing faith orientations as well.

Without work to hold a couple together, skills and habits of communication and intimacy became even more important. What kind of work patterns, then, might best cradle the intimate, egalitarian marriage that had become such a norm in our culture? That was the question we and many others faced. Resolving it was an intricate challenge for us, first in the OIKOS Project, then in our work at Andover Newton Theological School, and finally in retirement, when work patterns fell away as a decisive constraint.

Because of this spotlight on the work-family interaction, the oikos framework also led to a period of special interest in business ethics from this perspective. In this work I emphasized how business ethics needed to move from a narrow focus on individual decision-making or corporate policy to a broader field of relationships with family order, faith, and ecology. In an article on the oikos framework in the *Journal of Business Ethics*, I argued that for the sake of broader social stability corporations should find ways to enable couples to function in their otherwise highly individualistic conception of work.[2] While there has been some progress in changing work-family relationships in the business world, it has been slow, particularly in the US, and we have much left to accomplish.

I also turned the oikos perspective on issues in religious education. In the article "Transformation at Work," in a volume edited by Allen J. Moore, I explored the changing relationship of work and family patterns to practices of religious education. In this case I turned to my concept of covenantal publicity to expose the way religious education can help people find public expression for their deepest understandings of trustworthy relationships—to God, themselves, their families, fellow citizens, and to the earth. The article called for a rigorous and critical engagement between the ways workplaces transform people for good or for ill and the kinds of transformation the church seeks to bring about in people's lives.

The OIKOS Project brought together my own personal experience of family reconstruction, transformation in personal identity, and vocational adjustment with my development as a theologian, ethicist, and ecclesiologist. With its entrée into both private and public worlds, the oikos perspective shaped a good deal of my subsequent thinking, teaching, and research. It reinforced my own early conviction that we think and act in terms of deep-seated emotional images through which we perceive our world and order our lives. Though it never gained a lot of traction in wider publics, it is a conceptual framework that still guides my thinking and communication to this day.

---

2. Everett, "OIKOS: Convergence."

Ministerial Education and the Doctor of Ministry Program

Doctor of Ministry programs emerged in the 1970s as part of an effort to strike a parity among the basic degrees in law, medicine, and theology—the classic three professions. Law schools moved to granting a JD correlative to the MD, but schools of theology were unable to put together an economically viable four-year program that would parallel the other two professions in combining classroom work and clinical training. The Doctor of Ministry became a post-graduate degree after the Master of Divinity for people established in ministerial settings.

My own development, with my deep interest in ecclesiology, worship, and the complex relationships among practices, theories, and loyalties, disposed me to the kind of practical theological work at the core of Doctor of Ministry programs. While growing attuned to the work of ministry in a Roman Catholic environment in Milwaukee, I taught some adjunct DMin courses at McCormick Theological Seminary in Chicago and also at Mundelein, the Seminary of the Roman Catholic Archdiocese of Chicago. In taking on directorship of Candler's DMin program, I was able to articulate a theological and educational rationale for it to guide us.

In addition to the DMin, I was also Candler's director of their doctoral program in pastoral care and counseling. I also was serving half-time as Associate Professor of Ethics and Ecclesiology. It was a happy though often hectic pairing of practical administrative work with my research and teaching activity. It was also an invitation to spread myself over too broad a range. It still amazes me that I added on regular OIKOS Project presentations, an effort to convene a network of faculty concerned with family studies, and also active participation in Emory's emerging Religion and Law program. In a large, fragmented university setting, my instincts for connecting things was also stretching me beyond my personal resources.

What linked all these things together was a focus on the education of professionals who were trying to marshal deep theoretical resources (theology, psychology, jurisprudence, sociology, and administration) in the service of persons and communities. In the Doctor of Ministry program I set forth the model of the minister who is also a teacher ("doctor") of ministry through example, instruction, and supervision. This was more than the learned ministry of my Calvinist heritage. It was the disciplined and theologically informed teaching and supervision by which church leaders might grow in personal faith and ecclesial leadership.

This emphasis carried over to an expanded interest in the field of church administration, where I applied some of the work I had done in *Disciplines in Transformation* as well as in the OIKOS Project to the particular context of churches and congregations. It was practical ecclesiology with a distinctive perspective and methodology. In particular, it demanded that institutional leaders take into account the governing images they and their constituents brought out of their various oikos settings and which shaped their behavior in the church and other publics. It also required a critical self-awareness of the way their patterns of leadership were shaped by the way they related their theological approaches to the sociological and psychological practices and perspectives required for effective leadership in large organizations. This, at least, was the thrust of my teaching, even if it may not have reached all my students or even satisfied my own goals.

In the midst of this work at Emory, I became involved in a North American effort funded by the Lilly Endowment to strengthen Doctor of Ministry programs. My increasingly deep involvement in the late 1980s led to my becoming the founding President of the Association for Doctor of Ministry Education, which held annual conferences to bring together directors of programs and others in order to pursue this work more effectively. It is still continuing its work twenty-five years later. In my retirement I am part of a large and vital United Methodist congregation with over fifty retired clergy and church workers. I often feel as if I never left the Doctor of Ministry work I started so many years earlier!

Religion, Federalism, and the Struggle for Public Life

The struggle for public life has been a major theme in my work, beginning with my formation in Washington and winding through my inquiries into psychology, family, ecclesiology, and constitutionalism. In some sense, we are always drawn to study things that we think are important but that we don't understand and aren't very good at. As an intellectual and in many ways a strong introvert, the dissonance between my moral vision and the world around me drew me into a life of trying to bring moral ideals and practical reality into better alignment.

Over the years of wrestling with this ethical task, I came to see life as a struggle for covenantal publicity, even though my own psychology and physiology made me unsuited for the rough and tumble of political conflict and negotiation. For me, woodworking was always a primary model for this crafting of order in conflict. My woodworking was an effort to fit a plan to the vagaries of wood's grain, figure, and malleability. For Sylvia, her work in visual art was the mode of her publicity. While for both of us our work was essentially a personal, private, and small group enterprise, it constantly impinged by its very nature on the publics in which it gained its wider meaning. For me, ecclesiology formed a middle ground between this personal spiritual work and the wider publics of political life. For her it was her artistic work in the church's public worship that formed that middle ground.

In joining the Emory faculty I asked that my title reflect the growing importance of ecclesiology in my work. Thus, I became an Associate Professor of Ethics and Ecclesiology. Even as ecclesiology came to greater prominence in my academic work I also moved to a closer conversation with law through my association with John Witte, who was giving shape and energy to Emory's Religion and Law program. His colleague in this work was Harold Berman, whom I had met during my graduate days at Harvard while studying with his good friend James Luther Adams.

Arising out of the ferment created by my work in *God's Federal Republic* and in the OIKOS Project, I began to focus on the intersection between federalist political theory, ecclesiology, and the public sphere. The OIKOS Project as well as my work on marriage and family in *Blessed Be the Bond* had brought my interdisciplinary method and key concepts of covenant, publicity, the oikos, and social differentiation to bear on the private and interpersonal world. Now, I wanted to turn a similar set of lenses on the interplay of religion and political institutions in the public world that was rapidly changing as we neared the end of the twentieth century.

It can be said that both Communism and liberal democracy have been efforts to organize large groups of people beyond the old bonds of ethnicity that had forged the basis of the fascisms that tore the world apart in mid-century warfare. With the collapse of the post-war confrontation between Communism and liberal democracy (remember my high school thesis about *The Daily Worker*?), communities, nations, and regions had to find new ways to organize themselves beyond the biologically grounded models of kinship, ethnicity, race, or gender roles. This quest informed the OIKOS Project just as it was shaping my inquiry into relationships of religion and political order.

In 1988 I made the first of two trips to South India, the second extending to a term teaching at United Theological College in Bangalore in 1991.

I became immersed in the complex and torturous history of the church in India's struggle for independence and a modern constitution. On my first visit I met Thomas Thangaraj, whom Candler had invited to be a guest professor for three years. He ended up staying at Candler for twenty, becoming a major guide and companion for me into all matters Indian and Christian.

In 1991-92 I spent ten months in Heidelberg, Germany, teaching at the university with my old friend from Lutheran World Federation days, Wolfgang Huber. At the same time, I worked out of the nearby church-affiliated research center (Forschungstätte der Evangelischen Studiengemeinschaft) that had hosted me in 1976, when I also taught two classes with Yorick Spiegel, whom I had met at Harvard, at the Goethe-Universität in Frankfurt. Wolfgang had already spent a semester with me at Emory in 1989, just as the Berlin Wall fell, doing some co-teaching and working on a major book on law and theological ethics. When not teaching with him in Heidelberg, I engaged in research into the role of the church in the tumultuous events surrounding the collapse of the East German state and its reunification with West Germany. Gerd Decke, with his deep engagement in German churches at the local as well as international level, helped introduce me to people and congregations on both sides of the Wall that had divided Germany from 1961 to 1989. Gerd, who had translated a condensed edition of *God's Federal Republic* into German,[3] was able to identify persons and organizations to visit that might help deepen and expand my research. His deep knowledge of my own work enabled me to reflect with greater nuance on the church's involvement in building up a re-united German federal republic.

At the same time, I was increasingly drawn into ecclesiological issues in the United Methodist Church in the United States. On my return from Germany, colleagues at Candler became involved in a study project on Methodist ecclesiology led by Russell Richey at Duke Divinity School, whom I had first gotten to know many years ago as a classmate at Wesleyan. Working with my Candler colleague Thomas Frank, I fleshed out how my federalist themes might help Methodists gain greater clarity about the nature of their "connectional" form of church organization. This venerated concept, stemming from the commercial world of Wesley's England, had already led to a very confused and expensive court case involving a United Methodist retirement home in California named Pacific Homes.

---

3. Everett, *Gottes Bund.*

This celebrated case became one of the case studies in my emerging book on religion and federalism.

Finally, my re-anchoring in the southern Appalachians, with the building of a retirement home in the Great Smoky Mountains north of Atlanta, awakened a deeper sense of the culture of the Cherokee, who had been forcibly removed from that land in the 1830s under the policies of President Andrew Jackson. The anomalous Constitutional position of Native American "nations" and the failure to incorporate them into the emerging federalism of the American republic posed key questions for my inquiry into the contemporary relationship between religion and public institutions. All of these experiences began to shape a major book-length inquiry that emerged in 1997 entitled *Religion, Federalism, and the Struggle for Public Life: Cases from Germany, India, and America*.

The relationships among the constitutions shaping the three federal republics of Germany, India, and the United States and the organizational structure of their religious groups came to the center of this inquiry. Drawing on the framework in *God's Federal Republic*, I sketched in the characteristics of a public embedded in these struggles for self-governance. Four key questions organized my inquiry:

How might religion legitimate or de-legitimate this struggle for a fuller public life, especially the constitutional forms to cradle this life?

What patterns of differentiation between religious organizations and political institutions best foster a richer public life?

How do religious organizations mediate back and forth between the social world of religious adherents and the political spheres in which they seek a fuller "covenantal publicity"?

Finally, through what symbols, rituals, and habits of life do religious groupings mobilize people for wider public life?

These are the questions I was posing within the context of my experiences in India, Germany, and the United States. They would be explored through the kind of case study I had engaged in with my college thesis and with my work with the Lutheran World Federation.

The Churches and Germany's "Peaceful Revolution"

Thanks to my friendship with Gerd Decke and my consequent friendship with his senior colleague Ulrich Duchrow in the Lutheran World Federation, as well as my work with Wolfgang Huber, I felt I was somewhat prepared to study the complex issues and events of the "Peaceful Revolution" that united the former eastern and western German states.

As an American Protestant many of my theological roots lay in German theology. Jonathan Edwards stood beside Friedrich Schleiermacher, Roger Williams beside Karl Barth. H. Richard and Reinhold Niebuhr melded significant streams in both theological cultures. However, I had never worked through the disjunctions and tensions between the two traditions. In Germany's great "Turning" (*die Wende*) of 1989-90 the conjunction of European-style church "establishment" with American democratic enthusiasm and voluntarism offered a way to explore how my own theological commitment to dynamics of covenantal publicity might be tested in the surging waters of long-awaited liberation from the imprisoning vice of the Cold War. I was to discover even more than I expected.

The first part of my inquiry employed the concept of covenantal publicity as a tool of inquiry into the role of churches in fostering the revolutionary re-unification of the German Democratic Republic (the Deutsche Demokratische Republik, or DDR) and the Federal Republic of Germany (the Bundesrepublik Deutschland, or BRD). I then explored the fitful presence of covenant thinking and federalism in German history, in which a group of kingdoms were held together under the tent of the Holy Roman Empire and then a Prussian hegemony that unified them under a single king or kaiser. Apart from the brief life of the Weimar Republic, Germany had never experienced the federalist conjunction of states under a constitution that shaped my thinking in the US. It was only after the cataclysm of the Nazi era, with its centralized, totalitarian state, that the sectors under American, British, and French control sought to create a properly federal political order that would check future attempts to centralize state power. It was called the Bundesrepublik Deutschland. In German, the word for covenant, *Bund*, could be carried directly into its federal meaning.

In some sense this federalism was an import. Germany had a limited, though not non-existent, culture of covenant-making under monarchical rule of earlier centuries, the Hansa League being probably the most famous. Moreover, the churches were closely accommodated to the legal and bureaucratic forms of the state, including its finances. The impulses of voluntary association by covenanted church bodies could scarcely penetrate this long-established ecclesiastical shell.

However, there were new impulses in the post-war era. The memory of the persecuted "Confessing Church" of Dietrich Bonhoeffer and others beckoned to a more independent, voluntary church model. The model of the World Council of Churches, echoed in Germany's Council of Evangelical Churches (EKD), offered a further conciliar, covenantal form that might in turn lay down a culture redolent of biblical covenanting. Though the early form of the EKD embraced the Evangelical Churches in all the sectors of occupation, the eastern churches were finally forced to form their own federation (*Bund der Evangelischen Kirchen*) parallel to the western council of the EKD. (They reunited after the reunification of the two countries.) Nevertheless, the eastern churches preserved a certain autonomy over against the state. In fact, it was the heritage of state-like ecclesiology that gave them a privileged place within the atomized public of the East German state. In their constrained autonomy they could begin to nurture a small public space that burst forth with the withdrawal of Soviet control.

In these little publics of the churches of the DDR, issues of peace and ecological degradation could be aired in prayer, worship, and discussion. I called this church public a "*Kern der Öffentlichkeit*"—a nucleus, or seed, of the public—struggling to find expression in the wider society. The DDR had been a "democratic republic" that related individuals to the state in such a way that it could be neither democratic or a republic. In these little publics people were starting to learn what it was to create and share a public life.

This came to dramatic vitality in the collapse of the old state, as people assembled around round tables to hash out their experiences, claims, and opinions for shaping a new order. The roundtable movement, similar to what Hannah Arendt had called "the councils of the people,"[4] was the stage for this emerging new public order. The roundtable became for me, as it had for many Germans, the symbol of this longing for a more viable and just republic. It came to form a crucial symbol for me in future years.

Once I could identify this germination of new public orders, I turned to the need for new covenants to shape and secure them. In *God's Federal Republic* I had worked with a framework of the three covenant partners: God, people, and land. Germany offered struggles over the identity of all three. With their concept of God, Germans inherited a God as "*Landesherr*," a patriarchal care-taker of the country. Its distorted and demonic form had been the tyranny of Hitler and the faceless state of Communist control. While the "crucified God" of Lutheran piety, recently revivified in new ways

---

4. Arendt, *On Revolution*, esp. 252.

by Jürgen Moltmann,[5] offered the usual counterpoint to this patriarchal ruler, it was God as liberator and liberating Spirit that was needed in the ferment of this so-called peaceful revolution. This, I found, was a weak partner in the emerging new church public. German suspicion of any concept or symbol that might be twisted into a triumphalism led by a charismatic leader constantly eroded any version of this liberating God that could be turned into its demonic shadow.

One of the major catalysts for the emergence of the church public in the 1980s in the DDR was the realization of the deep ecological degradation caused by the economic decisions of the Communist regime. The integrity of the land and the renewal of a politics of public accountability found a flowering in the Conciliar Process for Justice, Peace, and the Preservation of Creation that the churches conducted in 1988-89. The revolution thus began with a struggle for a new covenant with the land.

Finally, Germans had to come to a new sense of peoplehood that left behind the image of a monolithic ethnicity in favor of a more pluralistic conception based on the commitment of equal citizens to a constitutional republican order of free public argument and negotiation. Some of the first issues in the newly re-united German republic was the status of immigrants and refugees, the terms of citizenship, and the shape of religious freedom in education and relief work, all of these issues too technical to rehearse here. In any event, all the issues from the American experience that had concerned me at a more theoretical level now burst into view, but with their own historical roots and possible developments. It was an absorbing and often exhausting work of discovery and reflection.

Even as the earlier themes of public, land, covenant, ecclesia, and constitutionalism were infused by this study with new meaning, another theme emerged that became central in the coming years—the work of reconciliation. The harm generated by an oppressive state had to be made right if a united Germany were to emerge as a renewed republic. As with so many things in Germany, it started with the files. If there is any single theme characterizing this revolution it was the turning from darkness to light. The vast state security system (the *Staatssicherheitsdienst*—the "Stasi") contained mile after mile of files that had to be released into the light of public inspection if people were ever to begin trusting each other again. And indeed, many lives, marriages, and relationships were lost to the searing light as well as to the guilt and retribution this opening unleashed. Just as Germans,

5. Moltmann, *Crucified God*.

beginning in the 1960s, had come to struggle with exposing and coming to terms with the Nazi horror, so now they had to seek the light of reconciliation within the shadow of yet another totalitarian night.

Johannes Gauck emerged from his work as a Lutheran pastor to guide the examination of the Stasi past. For some, the discovery was seen as the beginning of legal action to restore the rights and reputations of citizens. For others, it had to lead to an even broader re-covenanting to form a public life that would never again lead to this kind of reign of suspicion, terror, and ecological degradation. This was my first taste of the work of truth and reconciliation that would occupy my work in South Africa.

Religious Organizations and Constitutional Justice in India

In 1988, thanks to the intermediation of my fellow ethicist Max Stackhouse, Sylvia and I went to South India to attend some educational events in Madras (now Chennai), Salem, and Madurai. I had known Max, a close associate of James Luther Adams, since my graduate days at Harvard and we shared many of the concerns about covenant and voluntary association that feed into my work. My host in India was J. T. K. Daniel, a mathematician, theologian, and church educator. While only a three-week visit, it opened my eyes (and ears, nose, and mouth!) to the dense variety of Indian culture as well as to its Christian traditions. We returned in 1991 for a five-month stay while I taught at United Theological College in Bangalore. On that second visit Sylvia immersed herself in artistic work with Jyoti Sahi, one of India's leading religious artists, who has continued in conversation with us to this day. I began digging into my research on religion and federalism in India.

India has long been the test case for the struggle between status and contract as the defining framework for social life. Henry Maine, whose concepts shaped succeeding understandings of this struggle, was a key counsel to the British government in India in the nineteenth century. From the standpoint of my study, "status" pointed to the world of caste and patriarchy, "contract" to the world of publics, covenants, and federal order. Caste and patriarchy were also embedded in the classic social world of varna-ashrama-dharma, that is, the order of color (varna), stage of life (ashrama), and rules of just living (dharma). What Westerners came to call the "religion" of Hinduism was deeply involved in legitimating this order. It was a life of what I called "geo-piety" (an attachment to place) and "bio-piety" (an

PRACTICES

attachment to the conditions of birth, such as sex, race, color, inheritance and the like). Islam, Christianity, and Buddhism were always foreign insertions into this fabric of Hindu life. Islam had been the religious culture of an imperial rule under the Moghuls in earlier centuries. Christianity had been, under the British, sometimes a puppet, sometimes, a modernizer, and sometimes, as with the Malabar coast, practically a sub-culture of its own. Now India was faced with the question of whether these religious traditions could make a positive contribution to anchoring the constitutional world of a federal republic.

All of these traditions created a skein of pluralism in Indian life. Pluralism was no stranger to India, but the political pluralism underlying republics and federal orders was far from developed when India set out to become a modern federal republic after independence in 1947. At independence, India faced the daunting challenge of developing a constitutional republican order in a culture that offered little foundation for it. B. R. Ambedkar, the new constitution's chief architect, was a jurist trained in the US and the UK, a member of an oppressed caste in Rajasthan, and, eventually, a Buddhist in protest against Hindu caste ideology. The Roundtable Conferences in London in the early 1930s had laid some of the groundwork for this constitution, at least from the standpoint of the British governing elite and their Indian collaborators, but the actual constitution that emerged had to deal with the peculiar mixture of religion, caste, and patriarchy that had infused Indian culture for millennia.

Much of this intransigent milieu was dominated by what has been called Hindu communal nationalism. If there was to be a stable constitutional order, it would have to be rooted in the ancient religion of the Hindus, which was increasingly represented by an extreme form that led to the departure of Muslims from the Indian National Congress before independence and to the bloody and traumatic partition of the country in the wake of independence. This violent division and the communal violence that has dogged the country ever since pose the question of how the secular constitutional order can deal with the schismatic forces of a varied land, the bonds of caste, and the rigid walls of communalism to build a federal polity of publics that can negotiate the turbulent waters of modernization.

To investigate this interaction I turned to three famous civil cases that seemed to crystallize these dynamics. The first was the case of Soosai, a Christian cobbler in Madras, whose occupation put him among the former outcastes of India. In most of India lower caste and outcaste Indians had converted to Christianity to escape the Hindu caste oppression that reduced them to the circumstances of their low birth. The Constitution of 1950 contained articles that called for special actions to redress this historic inequality through a process that came to be called "compensatory discrimination." Soosai, as a member of an outcaste group, sought to use some special housing provisions under this act. Because he was a Christian, the court argued, he was not allowed to use this provision because he was no longer a Hindu and therefore had become casteless, according to the dictates of the Christian church. Thus, the categories of biological communalism were imposed on a religion that did not accept them and robbed one of their members of a right that flowed from a supposedly secular constitution. Rather than being seen as a citizen under the Constitution of India, he was forced to choose between being a Christian, and losing that right, or converting back to Hinduism in order to gain it.

This mind-numbing incongruity brought to the fore once again the clash between biologically-grounded status and egalitarian citizenship under the law essential to a constitutional order. The tension between the biological appeals in "body thinking" and the voluntarism of a genuine public life had taken on yet another costume in the parade of thought flowing from this distinction.

The second case took up the plight of Shah Bano, a Muslim woman who had been divorced by her husband using the "snap divorce" widely rejected by Muslim leaders. According to statutory norms, she was to be properly awarded with alimony in order to avoid a state of destitution. However, to enforce this law would have pitted the state against the religious "personal code" that was to be enforced by a Muslim Board, not the state. Marriage under the British Raj was placed under boards controlled by the various religious groups. It was not a civil matter. Even Christians had to marry (and divorce) according to a separate law based on practices in the English church in the nineteenth century. Under provisions of the 1950 Constitution, a separate law of civil marriage was instituted, but very few either knew about it or, because of social pressure, took advantage of it. The illiterate Shah Bano was powerless before her communal authorities. Here, bio-piety took on both its patriarchal and its communal face.

In addition, the case asked the question of whether Indian federalism was constituted by distinct geographic political entities (the states) or by religio-communal groups. Indeed, would the freedom of these groups to control their internal affairs (among them marriage, family, and inheritance) immunize them from the democratic ethos of the Constitutional state? Who, indeed, are the appropriate partners in the covenant that constitutes a federal order? This question would return in force in an American case study. It contained not only the question of federal constituencies but also of what values should be at play in a religious organization. That is, what are the normative ecclesiologies not only for the Christian church but for other religious groups? And how should the civil order be related to these ecclesiological forms? Before leaving the Indian scene, I addressed these questions in a final case, that of the Basel Mission.

The Basel Mission was established by Swiss Christians for missionary work in India, not in order to found a church per se. However, over time it did indeed become a regularly established Christian organization of worshipping congregations. When the Church of South India was formed in 1947 these congregations sought to join it but were sued by a dissident group who claimed that their "right to worship" had been injured by this move. Under law stemming from the British era, they had a right to sue in civil court to redress this "injury." Indeed, this law, in spite of the secular constitution under which it exists, has been invoked in church conflicts often in the late twentieth century. The state, then, must perforce be dragged into settling not only property disputes but also questions of doctrine and worship.

In its ultimate ruling (twenty-six years later!) the High Court separated out these matters of doctrine and worship from the organizational matters and held against the plaintiffs because this was just an organizational matter to be solved by the law of trusts, not theological disputation. Indeed, even the question of episcopacy and internal democracy was merely an organizational rather than a theological matter. In the process, of course, it neatly severed what churches always want to hold together, namely, the body of their organization and the spirit of their faith and worship. Only an ecclesiology separated from theology could function in the Indian legal system.

The Basel Mission case also lifted up the peculiar meaning of religious freedom in Indian law. While Hindu traditions are highly communal, the worship of individuals—their puja— can be highly individual and idiosyncratic. Thus, "worship" can be individual, but it occurs within a tight communalism governing every aspect of behavior. Moreover, because of the communal character of religion, "freedom of religion" can be interpreted as freedom from solicitation for conversion, that is, from the proselytization that was indispensable to the rise of Christianity in India.

Freedom of religion for Christians means not only the freedom to convert and be free agents religiously but also the freedom of their churches from state interference. For Christians in a constitutional state, the church is inherently an association of individuals, not a communal group as such. Thus, we see here two very different understandings of the "individual" and his or her freedoms, not to mention two different understandings of the proper organizational form of religion.

These case studies from India, with their very different cultural contexts and histories, lifted up, often in new ways, some enduring themes. First, we need to remember the way that the associational view of religion is the natural companion to republican constitutional orders. Communal versions of the church threaten not only key tenets of Christianity but also the integrity of the constitutional order. Secondly, we have to be clear about the constituent publics that constitute a federal order. They have to be seen as genuine publics or republics that are federated by negotiation and covenant-like agreement. They cannot simply be a collection of ethnic and communal groups. Third, the individual who is ratified in baptism in the church is ultimately an associational individual liberated in many ways from communal ascriptions and biological statuses. It has taken Christianity in the West almost two millennia to reach this point, but this claim is deeply embedded in the Church's original faith. This is a theme rooted not only in my Baptist and Independent ancestors but in the natural interplay of constitutional republicanism and democracy with the church. This core conviction found additional flowerings in some of my later intellectual and practical work involving feminism and civil and ecclesial rights for sexual minorities.

The Indian cases lifted up something that had emerged in the German study. Constitutional stability and renewal require deep-seated works of reconciliation. As I said in this study, "Reconciliation of estranged groups is necessary for a federal republic that seeks widespread democratic participation."[6] This is much more than compensatory discrimination or affirmative action. It requires patient truth-seeking in face-to-face publics searching for common ground for the sake of a more just civil life.

---

6. Everett, *Religion, Federalism*, 103 and 164–67.

PRACTICES

Sacred Lands and Religious Assemblies in America

Finally, I turned to my own country to look at two civil cases that lifted up issues of ecclesiology, constitutional order, and federalism. Rather than referring to the United States of America, I referred to this federal order as America, because the question of the place of the Native American "nations" has never been resolved in our land. Thus, to refer to the United States of America blinds us to the actual federal issues within this country.

The somewhat myopic view of America I had known as a boy growing up in Washington, DC, had now expanded to seeing our own national story as part of the great American continent, the last to be settled by the humans who had arisen in the great rift valleys of Africa. I had become aware that I lived on a fault line between the first settlers, from the West, whose arrowheads still turned up in the fertile fields at the farm, and those from the East, not only my forebears to New England but also those who brought enslaved Africans to work those very fields. The story of my America now exposed its origins in settler invasion and enslavement of Africans seized in the slave trade. Awareness of this expanded story informed this book but it would take another ten years to find literary expression in my historical novel *Red Clay, Blood River*.

For my intellectual ancestors, the New World was a tabula rasa on which they sought to write their covenantal visions of a new order that would endure for the ages. As Donald Akenson points out in *God's Peoples*, this meant that an associational society grounded in covenants and constitutions was seeking to be planted in the fertile ground of an undefined wilderness. However, as my teacher Robert Bellah wrote in *The Broken Covenant*, its origin in slavery and invasion meant that the covenants binding us to a larger divine purpose of justice were broken from the beginning. From the standpoint of my Baptist heritage, the refusal of baptism to these enslaved people, with its traditional sign of wider citizenship, was only one symbol of the impact of this brokenness in my Christian heritage. Like the settlers' broken treaties with the Native Americans, the broken covenant to care for the earth itself was yet another. It was only very recently that I finally read *A Key into the Language of America* (1643), by my distant ancestor Roger Williams, who tried to understand and respect the language, culture, and land rights of the Native Americans who saved his life after he was banished from Massachusetts Bay. The struggle has been in my very bones, though it has taken a lifetime to realize it.

Making My Way in Ethics, Worship, and Wood

The covenantal form of association promoted in this wild land was truncated to a confederacy among the patriarchs of the plantation South of slavery, while it was reduced to mercantile contract between capitalist owners and industrial workers in the North. I grew up along the Potomac, drinking from both wells. Reciprocally, the Southern patriarch joined with Northern shippers to sell and transport human beings into slavery. The mercantile chieftains of the contractual world exercised their patriarchal powers over women, workers, and families alike. The world they built powered the engine of revolution and then ran into the destruction of the Civil War, whose battlefields I traversed on many a visit with my father.

Indeed, the Civil War, as I had already pointed out in *God's Federal Republic*, was a contest over whether the American constitutional order was a severable contract based on the self-interest of the partners or an indissoluble covenant rooted in a divine purpose straining toward greater justice, participation, and happiness. As I learned in my teens, Edward Everett, also part of my family tree, had run on a third-party ticket, the Constitutional Union party, in 1860 with the future Confederate leader John Breckinridge to try to avert the sundering of the nation. It is not surprising that constitutionalism became such a central preoccupation in my intellectual life. That my forebears were passionate about defending it may have left in me a sense of its inherent fragility in the face of economic interest, ethnic passions, and their own appeals to biological or religious superiority.

From the perspective of covenantal publicity there was another form of brokenness as well. The publics that arose far from baron, prince, and monarch were restricted to propertied white males. The idea of a republic grew indeed from a small bruised seed. I was aware from an early age of the plurality of peoples in the world, in spite of the racial segregation that characterized my milieu. That my drive to church down Massachusetts Avenue in Washington passed numerous embassies and that people of many races and religions all showed up in my everyday life were normal parts of my experience. Perhaps it was this plurality, essential to Washington's political life, that fueled my commitment to the open publics inextricably joined to my understanding of covenant and constitutionalism. The upheavals of my twenties further clarified the restricted character of the publics which I, like my country, had grown up with.

This plurality, as much as the rejection of monarchy, made constitutionalism necessary. As my reflection continued later in a more theological vein, I came to understand better how the division of authority within the modern constitutional orders (the "separation of powers") also mirrored a division of authority within the Trinity. Such a complex transformation of the traditional notions of divine unity and governmental monarchy fed into my sense of the need to find firmer foundations for legitimating such a constitutional order. Our religious symbols needed to have a better engagement, a kind of shared language, with our actual political commitments in order to implement a more satisfactory order of justice in public life. They needed to occupy the same language world in order to speak critically to each other. This task had been at the heart of my effort in *God's Federal Republic*.

This search for a common language in which theology and political theory could argue with one another more effectively was rooted not only in a concern for the relevance of Christian ethics in the political world. It was also related to Robert Bellah's search for a civil religion that could legitimate a governmental order shorn of traditional religious connection. These two concerns became central to this study.

They led me first of all to the way the US Constitution's First Amendment sought to guarantee religious freedom and disestablishment of religion. On the one hand, the First Amendment tried to cut off governmental control of and dependence on an established church. On the other hand, it prohibited governmental interference in the unconstrained religious publics flourishing across the land. In short, it erected a hands-off separation between the religious and secular orders, something rooted in all of Christian tradition despite its perversion in the Constantinian era.

In these case studies I came to look more closely at the additional problem of legitimating a differentiated system of authority within this constitutional context. How, indeed, did the interplay of a pluralism of ecclesiastical systems play out within the world of a federal system of political authority? The monarchical model of a unified system of authority patterned after the patriarchal household had been drawn to a close, at least in government. What did this mean for the inherited monarchical orders of the churches?

All these concerns were reflected in the two cases I examined in this book. One arose in the United Methodist Church, in which I had become deeply involved. The other case arose in the life of Native Americans trying to resist the onslaught of commercial and governmental interests threatening their ancestral sacred lands. Their claims had become more vivid to me as I set roots down in the ancestral lands of the Cherokee.

Making My Way in Ethics, Worship, and Wood

The Pacific Homes Case

Pacific Homes was a Methodist retirement development in California that was set up in the era when people turned over most of their assets to residential institutions like this in exchange for the expectation of continuing care until death. Because people were living longer than had been expected, Pacific Homes eventually went bankrupt and offered a renegotiated agreement with the residents. Though most of them accepted it, a group of holdouts, urged on by their lawyers, sued Pacific Homes, the United Methodist Church, and other entities and individuals for over 600 million dollars. Though the trial court ruled for the Homes and other defendants, an Appeals Court reversed their ruling. Fearing more ruinous costs, the Homes and its sponsoring United Methodist Conference did not contest this ruling and settled out of court, paying out twenty-one million dollars to the plaintiffs and four million dollars to their lawyers. Other Conferences and entities in the UMC network loaned much of this money to the sponsoring Conference to enable them to meet this obligation. Because of the startling nature of the Appeals Court's opinion, I began mining it for what it might teach us about the interplay between ecclesiology and Constitutional law in the US.

I cannot go into the case's intricacies here. My purpose in this reflection is to tease out the aspects relevant to my effort to understand this interplay in the American context. In this case, the peculiar ecclesiology of the United Methodist Church was forced into a procrustean bed of judicial assumptions that a church was either hierarchical or congregational in its polity. The complex web of "connections" embedded in trust deeds and other mutual commitments was overridden to find that the UMC, which is neither of these options and which does not legally exist as a corporate person, was liable, like any hierarchical corporation, for the acts of its affiliated organizations. Like the India High Court in the Basel Mission case, the judges simply ignored the theological claims behind the UMC ecclesiology and treated it like a business corporation.

I should not be too harsh on the courts' rudimentary grasp of ecclesiological and theological issues, since the very discipline of ecclesiology within the Methodist churches had atrophied under the impact of an individualistic theology that could not grasp the way that church organization itself expresses fundamental theological values. Moreover, these values lead to organizational forms that may not fit the categories of secular law. This is another reason why the First Amendment had sought to curtail the courts' interference in religious life. When confronted by an actual incursion into an interpretation of the church's ecclesiology, the church lacked a solid basis for resisting the false alternatives of congregationalism and corporate hierarchy. The UMC was therefore unable to marshal a disciplined interpretation of its own connectionalism for the court. The court proceeded to reduce its organization to the same type as a hierarchical business organization and apply the law to it.

Here, in somewhat stark terms I saw in a new way what had preoccupied me in my doctoral dissertation about body thinking, namely the contest between the hierarchical organizational model legitimated in standard models of the body and the associational models of covenantal publicity and, in somewhat inelegant ways, the connectionalism of the UMC. The implicitly deep covenantal structure of the UMC lay outside legal forms and, to the extent it availed itself of the symbol "Body of Christ," it was a spiritual body not captured by legal forms. The Pacific Homes case was an example of the truncated understanding of federal order that had come to occupy the American legal order. Because the church could not mount a clear case for its version of a kind of covenantal, federal order different from the standard American account, it fell prey to the reduction of covenantal association to contractual obligation that cost the UMC's members so dearly.

The costly outcome of this case led the UMC to construct legal firewalls to insulate the various entities of the UMC from legal liability incurred by other parts of the church. Thus, the sense of being one "Body" in Christ was attenuated in order to accommodate American legal categories.

What was implicated in the case as well was the question of how the open and spontaneous publics necessary for the vitalization of a political order rooted in covenantal publicity could be protected within a constitutional framework. It is a question not only of the way the church can be a free public in a free republic, but also of how those free publics can generate a covenantal order that is expressed in Constitutional law while also reaching beyond it and beneath it. Is there a way of thinking about covenant and federalism that does not get sucked back into a simple hierarchical model? Indeed, does the doctrine of the Trinity, which itself has usually been reduced to the patriarchal pyramid of Father-Son-and vague feminine Spirit, provide some entrée into a more differentiated model of federal order as well as public life?

As I reflect on this study in 2021, I see how ill-equipped we are in my country to mediate the ferment of the little publics to the wider polity. Instead, established political parties have in many respects become unhinged from the actual federalist spirit as well as from deep covenants of mutual care for people, land, and the deeper purposes of our common life. As a result we are besieged by celebrity demagogues or dark money placeholders removed from the frame of covenantal publicity and the constitutional order erected two hundred years ago to try to hold together, even though very imperfectly, these two components of our life.

The Pacific Homes case lifted up tensions over Constitutional authority and ecclesiology, leading to a deeper reflection on what covenantal publicity might mean in the church as well as in political life. But there was yet another dimension opened up by my notion of the full covenant of God-people-land, namely, how contests over land and especially "sacred land" reverberated in the federal political order envisioned by the Republic's founders. My second American case developed this line of inquiry more fully.

Native American Sacred Lands

In 1990 we bought five acres of land on Wolfpen Mountain just outside Waynesville, North Carolina, and adjacent to the log house my old friend Jim Fowler had built for his retirement years. The home we built there eventually became the place where I have lived longest in my somewhat wandering life. Until 1791 this land was the ancestral hunting grounds of the people called Cherokee by the settlers. Indeed, as I came to know later, one of Sylvia's collateral ancestors had walked through the valley below our house in 1776 on the way to destroy Cherokee villages and their inhabitants and put them out of effective fighting for the British in the American Revolution. Before that, maybe some 8,000 years ago, some unknown mound builders had lived just across the ridge from us. Thus, my general awareness of the roles of native peoples in my life gained a tangible presence and intensified my interest in the issues of land, ownership, covenant, and the arduous task of reconciliation.

As I looked for a way into these issues, a recent Supreme Court case soon emerged to focus my thought. In the 1970s the US Forest Service proposed building a paved road through lands that several Native American tribes in northern California held to be their ancient sacred lands.

Practices

Representatives of the tribes formed a cemetery association in order to get standing in court to defend their sacred land. In *Lyng v. Northwest Indian Cemetery Protective Association (1988)*, the US Supreme Court ruled that this land, being the "property" of the United States, could be "developed" with a paved road without hindering Native American access to this land for their religious or cultic uses. From the standpoint of the Court, a portion of land could not itself be seen as a religious actor, such as a church, that could seek protection under the First Amendment to the US Constitution. Only specific actions constitute "religion" and only incorporated entities could present themselves as "persons" in court. These formulations raised a number of important questions about the nature of religion in America as well as of the nature of American federalism. Both of these bear on the understanding of covenantal publicity I was exploring in this book.

The concept of covenantal publicity helped me see ways that federalism goes well beyond the neat constitutional structure we usually attribute to a federal republic. Publics also overflow their legal forms, being linked together in many complex ways, including racial, ethnic, religious, and economic relationships. These little publics can be arrayed in a myriad of mutual pacts, understandings, and obligations. India, for instance, has been called a "compound federal republic" for this very reason. My inquiry into American federalism led me to see more deeply how Americans lived in an incomplete federal republic, since the relations between the national government, the states, and the Native American nations have never achieved a coherent form or a semblance of just relationships. The work of covenantal publicity is the life-blood of a federal republic, flowing through the many publics in which people seek to find an adequate expression of their lives and find confirmation in their covenantal bonds. Unless American constitutional frameworks could both nurture and be enlarged by these other publics, the life of covenantal publicity would never flourish for all Americans.

The US Constitution of 1787 had seen Native American tribes as foreign nations bound to the United States in treaties. This was reaffirmed in 1830 in the case of *Worcester v. Georgia*, itself a contest over Cherokee and state sovereignty. However, these same nations, the Court later declared, are dependent wards, not true sovereign states. The treaty relationship with them was eventually abolished in 1871. Our federal polity has seesawed between these two points throughout its 200-year history. Under the Dawes Act (1887), tribal lands were divided up into individual fee-simple parcels. Native tribes had been bound together in covenants with the land, but gradually the federal courts came to see Indian law and customs as "personal codes" attached to individuals rather than to a landed nation. In US Congressional efforts to reconstitute Indian nations in the 1930s, Native Americans started to claw back some of their collective powers, including their bond to the land.

In a religious protection case in the late 1970s the Court upheld the rights of traditional religions over against intrusive state laws prohibiting some of their practices, restrictions that had been going on for two centuries, especially in the prohibition of the Indian Ghost Dance practices at the end of the nineteenth century. That the protection of traditional communal tribal religions could also infringe on individual religious rights among Native Americans was an ironic consequence for those who had become Christians. The degree to which tribes could become full republics has remained a contested geography, but I did not pursue that inquiry. My interests here were driven more by the dynamics of covenant and publicity underlying legal forms.

As the tribes started to reassert their communal cultures, they had to find ways to represent their claims in the federal polity in terms that would fit the legal categories of the courts. The peculiar concepts of "land," "religion," and "tribal nation" represented the hardest cases. Just as for Native Americans land was not divisible into individual parcels that could be bought and sold in a market, so their religion could not be contained within the associational, corporate form of "church"—the dominant form of religion in American history and law. When religion and land formed one reality in Native American culture, the problem intensified. Land could not constitute a church. Indeed, the very concept of sacred land was restricted to cemeteries, which were sacred by virtue of the bodies buried there, or national memorials sacralizing certain events in (Euro-) American history. More recently, wilderness itself became a semi-sacred designation that removed land from the market and other uses. The *Lyng* case brought all of this into focus, including the tribes' decision to form a cemetery association to contest the desecration of their sacred land.

Biblical covenant had put land at the center of the covenant between YHWH and Israel. Legal development in Anglo-American history had deprived the land of covenantal status. Indeed, religion in the West had come to be a category of history, not geography or ecology. Divine revelation and divine-human relationships were known and worked out in history.

Faith was a historical matter of making, breaking, and renewing covenants among people. Any Christian reader of the Bible could see this, whether through the eyes of Dispensationalism's historic periods of Divine action, or the more sophisticated theories of religious evolution. For the historical mind, land was simply a neutral stage for human actors in publics and markets. For Native Americans, with a more cosmological and ecological understanding of land, it was the very life of the divine-human encounter.

My work on land ethics in 1979 had helped me see that ownership was a bundle of rights that could be parceled out into various relationships among people, including their political and economic organizations, and the land. Now I was looking at the ways land itself was not only a religious construct and reality but also had ambiguous relationships with the federal orders that tried to distribute various claims on the land. These various ways of relating to the land is what made America something that is more than the "United States." What it is would have to arise in a reconstituted covenant relationship between the descendants of settlers, of enslaved Africans, and the original peoples of the land, not to mention the very claims of the land itself for a sustainable and flourishing life. The latter, ecological, inquiry had begun in the OIKOS Project, but would await further development in the wake of this book.

In the *Lyng* case, the Court held that the land, while being a place for sacred rites, would have to yield to the Forest Service's desire to pave a road through it. Ironically, the subsequent designation under Federal law of much of this land as wilderness prevented the actual building of the road. What was important to me, of course, was the Court's reasoning as an example of the truncated grasp of covenant as well as the status of the Native American tribes as constitutive republics of our federal republic.

These strands of thought and questioning were not developed adequately either in my own thought or in the general conversation around federal republicanism and religion by the time I moved away from this research in retirement. However, it was sustained and developed in partial ways in my interest in the issues around Native American land claims, especially in my eco-historical novel, *Red Clay, Blood River*, as well as in my later work in ecology, liturgy, and worship.

Making My Way in Ethics, Worship, and Wood
Assessment, Evaluation, and Consolidation

I entered into this extensive study not only to employ my concepts of covenantal publicity as an analytical tool, but also because accumulated experiences and personal relationships in America, Germany, and India invited me into this story of their own political and religious history. Moreover, I wanted to see if I could go beyond an analytical stance to a constructive statement about the way we should understand the role of the church in a pluralistic world of developing federal republics. What forms of religious organization are destructive of the federal republican project? Which are truly able to engage it as critic as well as catalyst? How are these critical and constructive engagements mediated by culture, law, and social practices, including forms of family and associational life?

It was clear that the transition from patriarchy, with its attendant monarchical rule, to associational and pluralistic forms of social and political life stood squarely in the center of these relationships. As with the earlier work in *God's Federal Republic* and *Blessed Be the Bond*, the struggles toward egalitarian marriage, democratic citizenship, and pluralistic centers of authority were central to my personal as well as public concerns. Personally, I was continuing to deepen a marriage of companionship and communion. Publicly, I continued to struggle to affirm a political order whose pluralism and constitutionalism could resist the pervasive pressures to strong-man dictatorship and totalitarianism. As I write this, we are struggling against these unjust regimes in our own republic as well as around the world, even as the persistent longing for equality and genuine citizenship continues to arouse our hope and commitment. Indeed, I find language of struggle all through the book, including the title. This is no vision of evolutionary development but rather of continuing conflicts anchored in fundamental human tendencies.

To resist these strains toward a resurgent autocracy, religion, and in particular the church, would have to emphasize the transcendence of God beyond any particular political regime, but at the same time, it would have to cultivate the autonomous assemblies of religious faith as seedbeds of expansive and vital publics. Religious groups would have to assert their autonomy without fleeing into alienation or isolation from the public world. This set of commitments resonated not only with the tradition I received through James Gustafson, James Luther Adams, and H. Richard and Reinhold Niebuhr, but stretched back through some kind of spiritual DNA to my New England forebears.

Practices

Ecclesiology continued to be the hinge pin between religious vision and political practice. I defined it as "the study of the systematic and institutionalized practices of people with reference to the sacred, the divine, the transcendent."[7] Moral vision and action did not flow through the individual actions of religious people but through the way they organized to actualize these visions and pass them on to successive generations. Ecclesiology arises because we are finite creatures in time. We do not stand at the end of history but always within it. Therefore, ecclesiology is always a historical as well as theological matter. This is why case studies came to the fore in trying to understand the significance of ecclesiology for political life.

These themes gained clear enunciation in Ernst Troeltsch's work, which also shaped H. R. Niebuhr and my own mentors. In this study I modified Troeltsch's types of Christian formation (church, sect, and mystical fellowship) to identify the main forms I analyzed. I called them communal, associational, and institutional ecclesiologies. Communal forms were embedded in ethnic, familial, and tribal bonds. Associational forms emerged as voluntary assemblies that go beyond the ascriptive identities of sex, race, caste, and ethnic group. Institutional forms, while they have voluntary components, are basically fixed in place by the existing social institutions and deliver religious services to a set group of members. Clearly, my own theology led me to place primary emphasis on associational forms in which the church or other religious group is independent not only of the state but of market corporations and communal groups. This struggle for engaged autonomy for the church and religion was a central theme in this study.

Associational ecclesiologies, like the political constitutionalism of federal republics, appealed ultimately to some kind of covenantalism. Both of them undergird the process of constitution-making that is crucial to the formation of federal republics. This connection had been worked out in terms of theology and political theory in *God's Federal Republic*. I wanted to know whether it was in some way essential to the cultural and religious basis of federal republics in general.

For this investigation the deeper and more expansive meanings of covenant in biblical and some church traditions became a critical tool for analyzing how federal republican orders dealt with land, with persons, and with visions of the ultimate grounding of things in God or a similar image of the transcendent. A theology of covenant became a critical tool for

---

7. Everett, *Religion, Federalism*, 151.

investigating these dimensions. In particular, attention to the expansive web of relationships embedded in theological notions of covenant helped me see the limits and weaknesses of constitutionalism in the face of ecological, social, and biological claims on the fragile promises of legal constitutions. These tensions have only intensified as I write this in 2021.

In addition, the distinction between hierarchical and egalitarian templates of covenant in these traditions could help sort out and evaluate these dynamics in political life. I came to see hierarchy not only in the sense of immediate control from the top but in terms of the reception of covenantal obligations over time, as each generation arises, matures, and passes from life. It is a hierarchy of reception of a tradition. All social life must find a way to transmit its patterns in the face of the inevitability of individual mortality. Covenantal thought also adds new dimensions to the meaning of egalitarianism beyond the simple legal equality it usually conveys. Mutual care, respect, exchange, conversation, negotiation, and persuasion all become part of the dense network that arises among equals. These dynamics are crucial to the viability of any appeal to relationships among equals. This perspective would appear more strongly in my subsequent work on restorative justice, circle conversations, and roundtable worship.

As I worked through the final stages of this study, I became aware of the many writings and research of the political scientist Daniel J. Elazar, at Temple University, whose four-volume work on covenant and federalism was emerging in those years. Elazar, in spite of the effects of childhood polio that confined him to a wheelchair, poured his prodigious energies and searching intellect into a project that showed the significance of these ancient Jewish concepts and practices, along with their Reformation expressions, for the federal republican project of the modern era. I got to know him while I was teaching in the Boston area. I was greatly saddened by his death, in 2000, just before he was to appear in a panel discussing his work that I organized for the Society of Christian Ethics annual meeting.

These covenantal practices feed directly into the work of publicity. Participation, pluralism, and persuasion can only occur within a covenanted commonality of commitment. The concept of covenantal publicity, which Elazar cited in his jacket comments for this book, anchored these connections in ecclesiology as well as in political theory. Both a vital ecclesiology and a federal republican vision had to nurture free publics where people could engage in the pursuit of truth, justice, and mutual care. This meant that genuine publics could not be captive to economic markets, as in the commercial malls that have dominated the landscape of suburbia until very recently. Nor could they simply be absorbed into government. Like wilderness, they needed to have a kind of independent status that could mediate transcendence into everyday life.

As I looked at the very different ways this dynamic of covenantal publicity was working out in different cultural contexts, I became increasingly aware of the ways Islamic traditions shared in some of this biblical heritage but also diverged from it. The question of the relation of Islam to the federal republican project hovered in the wings as I completed the study, only a few years before the attacks of September 11, 2001, burst upon our life. Since then, this question became more central with my deep involvement in a ten-year conference series on interfaith peace work.

Covenantal publicity as an analytical tool also cultivated a growing conviction that the church could and should be a proto-public in its internal life and in its environing society. In Germany, I saw the church as a seed or nucleus of public life. As a proto-public, the church could nurture persons as citizens engaged in covenant-receiving and covenant-making. In its life they could express their own convictions in prayer, confession, forgiveness, reparation, song, and mission engagements. These practices also could form them for the exercise of citizenship in specific political arenas. In this, I was only deepening and extending the meaning of voluntary, covenant-based churches in my own Baptist past into wider arenas.

In these ecclesial proto-publics, the symbols and rituals of worship could both legitimate wider constitutional patterns and also critique them, as when I would employ the notion of a fuller covenant to critique the truncated contractualism of federal republics dominated by capitalist corporations or strangled by the partisan politics of self-interested political parties. Specifically, church practices like Baptism and Eucharist could be construed as ritualizations of citizenship and table conversation crucial to vital republican life. Elaboration of the political importance of these practices would stimulate my later development of roundtable worship in the context of reconciliation and restorative justice.

Indeed, what each of these case studies taught me was the importance of reconciliation in the development of vital federal republics. The strain toward publicity ignites the demand from traditionally excluded groups for recognition in a fuller public where they can find a place at the table and join in decisions that affect them. This is the democratic impulse in republican life. In the process they have to move from warfare and antagonism to one of equality and persuasion. This is the work of reconciliation.

In reconciliation, participants need to affirm a common past, seek repair for the injuries sustained in previously unjust relationships, and forge a covenant about a common future. Reconciliation is intrinsic to covenantal publicity in history. While it frequently requires a miraculous intervention by events or charismatic leaders, it also depends on the slow and painstaking work of remembering, forgiving, and promising a new way of life.

With the completion of this study and this book, I had a sense that I had reached the completion of the second intellectual phase of my life. The first had been a work of ordering, sorting, and framing a complex world of many disciplines, perspectives, theories, and practices. This is what I did in *Disciplines in Transformation*. The second was the substantive phase of laying out a basic approach to this constellation of public and private action in marriage and family, ecclesiology, and public life. *Religion, Federalism and the Struggle for Public Life* was the culmination of this effort. While I would continue to be sensitive to the tasks of these two phases, it was time to move on to a new phase of practical implementation, especially in the cultural work of worship and the arts.

Covenantal Publicity and Reconciliation

In my work at Emory I learned both my strengths and limits as an administrator. I could develop relationships among many different disciplines—especially law, business administration, and family systems—and relate them to professional practices in ministry and the church. But I was not skilled in the subtle and sometimes crude power politics of academia. As I moved into my early fifties, a new Dean pushed relentlessly for Candler to abandon its DMin commitments. While I had cultivated deep connections with many of my colleagues, some of whom I had known since graduate school, I felt my work there had come to an end.

In 1994 I pursued an opportunity to move to Andover Newton Theological School, where I became the Herbert Gezork Professor of Christian Social Ethics. This move would bring me full circle back to the Boston area, where I had launched out on my career twenty-five years before. What added to the attraction of this opportunity was that Sylvia could become a resident artist in the School's newly-inaugurated Theology and Arts program. The opening to a closer collaboration in our work resonated with our earlier interest in strengthening the communion bonds of couples with a vocational collaboration. Moreover, my own academic interests were increasingly turning toward worship and the arts as crucibles of ethical formation and action.

My long-time interests in interdisciplinary collaboration took on a new configuration at Andover Newton in which the connections of theology and ethics to ministerial practice, worship, and the arts came to the center. Close relationships with the graduate theology program at nearby Boston College reinvigorated my interest in Catholic theology and ethics. At the same time Hebrew College, a center for preparation of Hebrew teachers (and later Rabbis), began a close collaboration with Andover Newton by moving their facilities to adjacent property on Andover Newton's hill in Newton Centre. Within this nest of relationships, the arts and worship began to form an even more important integration point for my thought and work. With Sylvia and others in the Theology and Arts Program, I could begin to unfold more of my aesthetic sensibilities, even though the academic and administrative demands on me curtailed most of the poetry that had burst forth in the early years of our marriage. At the same time, a new door opened into what was in part a further chapter of *Religion, Federalism, and the Struggle for Public Life* and in part a deepening of my efforts to connect worship to ethics and the arts.

South Africa: Reconciliation and a New Constitution

In the 1990s South Africa began to emerge from the vise of apartheid that had been strangling it since 1948. I did not have any experience that could have enabled me to bring these developments into my study on religion and federalism, but, with the encouragement of Gerd Decke and Wolfgang Huber I began corresponding with John de Gruchy, who had spent his life in South Africa documenting and participating in the church's resistance to apartheid and now its work in helping to build a new, more democratic republic. Indeed, because of this connection and his interest in my parallel work, John added his own comments to the jacket of *Religion, Federalism, and the Struggle for Public Life*.

We arranged for me to come to Cape Town in the first half of 1998. As it worked out, John had to take his sabbatical in England, trading his summer for an English winter, while we took over their house (and swimming pool). At the same time, I was in communication with Prof. Dirk Smit at the Theology School of the University of the Western Cape. Dirkie was a member of the Society of Christian Ethics, and interested in the theology of covenant as well as the relation of worship to ethics. We met at its annual meeting in Atlanta just before Sylvia and I departed for Cape Town, where I joined him for a semester of teaching and collaboration.

Through conversations at UWC, a historically Colored institution, and at the University of Cape Town, as well as travels to other locations, I plunged into the exciting, sometimes violent as well as hopeful events of the transition into a new political era. The Truth and Reconciliation Commission, chaired by Archbishop Desmond Tutu and Alex Boraine, had been set up by the new Constitution in 1994 and was in its third year of hearings. I became a part of a research team at UCT, led by Prof. James Cochrane, to document and analyze the relation of the TRC to religious groups.

As I explored this process of reconciliation in this demanding context I became increasingly sensitive to the role played by rituals of testimony, apology, forgiveness, and memorialization. I was once again acutely aware of the direct and indirect role of the churches in both legitimating the previous regime as well as in helping birth a new order. Once again, I could see in churches the seedbeds for the publication of people's lives as victims and citizens in the process of reconciliation and re-covenanting relationships in a new republic. I wrote several articles at that time that took up the role of symbols, memorials, and covenant-making in the work of building up a new order.

Among them was an article, "Seals and Springboks," about the work of re-constructing both the monuments of apartheid and the sports rituals that can both unite and divide the racial and economic groups in South Africa. Robben Island ("Seal Island"), long synonymous with exile and punishment, became a symbolic gateway into citizenship in the new South Africa, as thousands made their way through its somber prison halls to re-live the "long walk" to freedom of Nelson Mandela and others who had struggled against the apartheid regime. As laid out in the later film *Invictus*, the South African rugby team, the Springboks, moved from being a symbol of white supremacy to being a symbol of a shared struggle for national pride and unity.

My five-month stay in 1998 led to a number of successive visits and stays in the next fifteen years, establishing South Africa as a kind of second home akin to my numerous contacts in Germany. Sylvia resonated with the dry climate and rocky hills reminiscent of her early years in eastern Oregon and soaked up the many artistic opportunities we encountered.

The South African experience deepened my awareness of the profoundly historical dimension of re-covenanting. Moreover, the way that history takes on public imagery and story shapes how it can become a common basis for new covenants. Publicity demands the expression of the memories of victims as well as of perpetrators. The publication of these memories then starts insisting on some kind of conversion of people's outlooks and habits in order to effect the reconciliation that is both embodied in and shaped by new covenants. Remembering rightly takes enormous courage, rooted in the faith that this is in fact the divine work of redemption in action. In the multi-religious composition of the TRC, along with the charismatic leadership of Bishop Tutu, lay the deep and sometimes hidden bridge between religious formation and political re-formation.

My South African experience also stimulated a closer look at memorialization in America. Indeed, the deep parallels between American and South African history struck me continuously: the European settlement in the seventeenth century, the rise of slavery, and the burgeoning of a neo-Christian civil religion in both its oppressive and liberative forms. Some of these reflections would emerge in my later historical novel. More immediately, they led to examining the struggles for reconciliation in American life.

Reconciliation and the Vietnam War Memorial

Having been seared by the experiences of the Civil Rights movement and my country's horrendous war in Vietnam, I began to examine the role of the Vietnam Memorial in Washington, DC, in the effort to bring about some kind of reconciliation in my own land. Ironically, this research was prepared for a symposium in Germany convened by my Heidelberg colleague Hans-Richard Reuter in September 1998. Written and presented in German and published in 2002, I have only now translated it into English.

The war in Vietnam, like the civil rights movement, deeply shaped my world and perceptions, so it was long overdue for me to explore the way the suffering of that tragic overreach of American military power could be kneaded into the deep memory shaping American culture. Having spent so much time in my youth in the battlefields of Virginia, I was aware of how suffering can lead to the arrogance of victimage and vindication. It can also, as with slain brothers in Union blue and Confederate gray, lead to greater awareness of the deep duality of our motives, perceptions, and actions. The dedication of those who struggled for a fitting memorial for the American war in Vietnam was realized beyond most people's expectations in the stunning gray scar in the land that now attracts a million visitors a year to grieve, ponder, and renew their commitment to a more peaceful world. It enables us to remember, to open our hearts, and to move ourselves and perhaps even our people onto a higher ground. Suffering can unite and heal as well as estrange and embitter. A powerful memorial can be a theater of profound transformation.

As I write this, violent conflict has erupted around me about the memorials of Confederate leaders that were erected in the early twentieth century to legitimate the enforcement of racial segregation—our own American apartheid. Because we have not attended to the painful work of right remembering, repair, and reconciliation, we now have to confront these angry demons of our culture anew. Whether we can finally come to terms with this history, which calls our finest civil-religious ideals into question, is once more on the table. Perhaps being raised in the midst of these memorials in Washington, DC, and Virginia attuned me to these issues in a way that many other people are not. Here again is a contest between the covenantal publicity of free participants and the biologically rooted claims of patriarchy and paternalism, plantation and slavery.

Reconciliation as a Journey

The narratives of covenant and the struggle for a fuller republic arise in the gap between historical reality and ethical vision. The image of "journey" kept emerging as I worked with this tension and led me to write a paper in 2003 for the Society of Christian Ethics entitled "Journey Images and the Search for Reconciliation." In it I examined three classic journeys: The Cherokee "Trail of Tears," the "Great Trek" of South Africa, and Mao's "Long March" during the Chinese Civil War. Journey images lie at the heart of cultural scripts that enable people to interpret their current circumstances and justify actions to achieve an ethical vision. The Trail and Trek stories drew on biblical journeys of Exodus and Exile to shape their meaning. Mao's Long March drew in part on the seventh century (CE) story of the Buddhist monk Xuansang's journey to India to recover the ancient Buddhist texts in order to repristinate the Chinese Buddhism of his day. This story was highly mythologized in *The Journey to the West* by subsequent story-tellers, who extolled the virtues necessary to unite the country around a single religious narrative. Similarly, the Long March of Mao became the primary source of moral instruction for his followers as he sought to unify China and recover its historic greatness.

Journey stories connect personal and collective histories in order to create a social order as well as a meaningful personal life. They connect our daily step-by-step story to the larger story of our common history as peoples, nations, and a species. They put seemingly disconnected events and changes over time into a coherent story. My long-standing effort to connect the personal and the public found yet another expression in this inquiry. In studying how these narrative dynamics unfold, I identified eight types of journey stories, ranging from those of exodus and liberation to those of exile and removal, wandering, exploration, conquest and settlement, pilgrimage, quest, and homecoming. Each of them contains specific meanings for alienation, personal and collective virtues, and reconciliation.

The power of these stories of journey to shape the contours of possible reconciliation burst forth in a week-long presentation I gave at the Summer School at the University of Cape Town in January, 2002. Near the end of my survey of these stories, a man in the audience declaimed that he now understood why those who had left South Africa during apartheid and were now returning couldn't feel a part of the reconstruction being undertaken by those who stayed. They were operating out of two different journey stories. Nelson Mandela himself, who had been incarcerated most of the time, wrote his own story as "Long Walk to Freedom," a very different "walk" from those who had had to flee the country. The meaning of reconciliation for a person or a group is heavily dependent on their understanding of the journey they have taken through the world of bitter alienation, injury, and brute survival.

Journey and Place

These patterns of journey also had to be understood alongside an alternative set of images—those of place. While journey images are central to historical self-understandings, place images take priority in settled societies and ecological visions. Places may occupy the beginning or end point in a journey, and so they have an inherent connection as well as distinction. They also require not only a reconciliation among people but between people and the land. Thus, I turned back to the ecological concerns that had arisen in my exploration of land ethics as well as in the case studies in *Religion, Federalism, and the Struggle for Public Life*.

Stories of journey and of place are necessary to the process of reconciliation. In telling these stories we open ourselves up to the possibility of linking our stories together in a common story that takes us beyond the present conflicts immobilizing us. Specifically, how can we tie the historical stories shaping us to our images of the land? This is just one more version of the classic tension between religious visions rooted in history and those rooted in the timeless cycles of the land. Strangely enough, I had grown up in this tension between the history-bathed memorials of Washington, DC, and the planting, nurture, and harvest of our dairy farm in the fertile Loudoun Valley of Virginia. It is a tension that has always been at work in my own life as I long to live among the forests and farms while my head is also filled with civic concerns about the dramas of public life. It is also manifested in my movement back and forth between the work of material craft and that of writing, speaking, and teaching. In many ways this tension is the warp and weft of my life, one whose conflicts and contradictions I have never resolved. Nor, perhaps, should I.

Praying for God's Republic

God's Federal Republic was an exercise in symbol transformation in the dialogue between biblical theology and political theory. In light of that work I set my sights on exploring how the ordinary acts of worship in religious practice could be changed under the impact of this theological perspective. These thoughts finally found expression in the mid-nineties in a little book that I wanted to entitle "Praying for God's Republic." My publishers, however, changed the title to *The Politics of Worship* without even consulting me, because they feared a right-wing nationalist view of the title. When I finally recovered the copyright, I put out a revised edition on my website with the original title.

What would it look like to pass through the often treacherous waters of worship from the symbolic world of lords, kings, kingdoms, reigns, and monarchy to that of republics, constitutions, democracies, federations, and public life? Moreover, how would this be couched within the broad transformations of our cosmology and ecological awareness? Here is how my presentation and argument went.

PRACTICES

The Dialogue of Ethics and Worship

To respond to these questions, I first had to establish, as was my long practice, some guidelines for the dialogue. Worship, it had to be acknowledged, shapes our ethics, just as our ethics makes claims that shape our worship. Worship motivates and forms us toward certain ethical dispositions, such as gratitude, obedience, love, and forgiveness. Through its arrangement of space, furniture, and participants, it establishes paradigms of right order, whether they be those of patriarchal monarchy, councils of elders, schools of sages, or halls for theatrical performance. Worship itself is a form of drama that provides scripts and choreography that help us shape our life in meaningful ways incorporating key values and ethical orientations. Whether staged in the austere courtroom of robed judges or on the dazzling stage of rock stars, worship forms express and legitimate the key rituals that shape our lives.

Our ethics, conversely, can reshape our worship, in spite of the heavy hand of tradition and the reverence for antiquity that worship often instills. Feminist ethics were already leading to women exercising priestly leadership, to altering the heavily male-dominated language of worship, and evoking feminine images and teachings in Scripture and tradition itself. Ecological ethics was lifting up the importance of themes of creation, including ritual observances related to Earth Day or the Blessing of Animals. The human rights enunciated in United Nations declarations as well as the ongoing achievements of civil rights movements in the US, South Africa, and beyond were being celebrated regularly in churches.

This dynamic process of cross-critique and change was, once again, an example of the process of reciprocal transformation I had laid hold of in *Disciplines in Transformation* twenty years earlier. It remains an essential value in my thought and life.

The Purposes of Worship

I then enunciated an understanding of the purposes of worship. I pointed out that many people see the purpose of worship as motivational. It is to create an emotional experience leading, especially in evangelical and revivalist traditions, to fundamental conversion of our attitudes, beliefs, and behaviors. One of the mistakes of the Social Gospel and liberal tradition, I maintained, was to think of worship only in this form, as a "battery charger" for social activism. In my view, this had led to a neglect of worship and the failure of energy as well as vision in these traditions.

For those in the Calvinist tradition, broadly speaking, worship is primarily education. The church, as Calvin said, is a school in which we are to learn about "God's Word." The primary focus of worship is the sermon and, in its more Evangelical variants, the preacher. Moreover, the sermon ought to be a learned exposition of Scripture. The sanctuary becomes a bare auditorium. This Calvinist understanding even came to affect Roman Catholic life after Vatican II. I will never forget a student at St. Francis Seminary who introduced me to its ornate nineteenth century chapel filled with statues, paintings, and stained glass, only to declaim "We have to get rid of this bric-a-brac so we can hear God's Word." I said to myself, silently, "Take it over to the Baptist church. They're really starved for it."

The Catholic tradition he was attacking had entertained yet another purpose for worship, which I called representation. The purpose of worship is to re-present in symbolic form the central dramas, beliefs, visions, and persons shaping Christian faith. The "sacrifice" of the Mass is in some way a re-enactment of Christ's sacrifice. Baptism is a re-entry into the waters of the Jordan with Jesus. A wedding is in some way an entry into Christ's marriage to the church. Worship, in short, re-presents a drama in which we enter the cosmic drama of salvation.

Out of these three historic purposes I constructed the purpose that would guide my own deliberation, namely, that worship is a rehearsal of God's right order. By calling it a rehearsal, I brought in the elements of dramatic representation that I had absorbed in my experience in Roman Catholic life. In calling it a rehearsal, however, I was also stressing its preliminary character. We are engaged in a drama that will be continually re-formed and changed. Worship has an anticipatory, eschatological character that constantly subjects it to renewed transformation.

By emphasizing our focus on God's right order I invoked the biblical, especially New Testament, roots of worship. This was a right order that had to be explored, studied, envisioned, and reflected upon. It was something to be educated into, as my Calvinist ancestors would have said. In worship as rehearsal, worship's motivational power arises in the way we learn ritually and symbolically the habits and dispositions that orient us toward the anticipated life of God's ultimate purpose.

In the peculiar cultic activity of worship we consolidate the cultural bases for our efforts to construct and live out a pattern of life that seeks some congruence with God's right order. This incorporated my response to Germany's experience, in which the churches became proto-publics of the emerging democratic order in the former East Germany. This chain from cult to culture to polity was a concept that stretched back to my earliest work on ethics and worship. It was a perspective rooted not only in the Christian life I had participated in for my whole life but also in the sociological perspectives from Emile Durkheim, Max Weber, and my teachers, Talcott Parsons and Robert Bellah.

Political Theory as the Partner of a Theology of Worship

Such a conception of worship rested on the belief, drawn from biblical study as well as the history of the church, especially in Europe, that the conceptual partner for worship should be political theory more than the psychology, philosophy, or even anthropology that I saw dominating the discussions around me. If worship were to recover both its biblical-theological origins and its historic vitality, it would have to engage political theory. Most importantly, it would have to converse with political theory if it was to transcend its traditional patriarchal and monarchical forms to engage the federal-republican and democratic tradition. Otherwise, it would remain limited to the work of individual and small group conversion, and be mired, often unwittingly, in ethnic solidarities or captivity to the political and economic powers-that-be.

Surely, one would think, such an argument would have guided American worship development since America's own republican revolution. But it clearly had not. In a little essay I first wrote for *The Christian Century* and then revised for this book, it was important to ask why we had remained monarchists on Sunday in spite of our democratic commitments the rest of the week. As Brian Wren had argued in his influential book *What Language Shall I Borrow?*, I wanted to move our liturgical language from the "Kingafap" of traditional worship (Wren's rendering of King-God-Almighty-Father-Protector) to something less bound to the old feudal and monarchical order. However, unlike Wren, I turned to contemporary political theory rather than nature and psychology for my symbols.

To do this I pointed out that under the terms of American "separation" of religion and state, religion had become a private matter sustaining personal health, family, friendship, and local congregational life. In exchange for their freedom from state interference, churches would not seek either to provide legitimation for the state or to control its policies. The symbols of patriarchal monarchy within this new republican state then fit neatly into the defense and celebration of the bourgeois family of the nineteenth century, with Christmas, complete with Hallelujah chorus, being its most precious festival.

The feminist critique of patriarchal symbolism, along with the exodus of women from the task of full-time household maintenance, began to erode this religio-familial construction. However, without a robust political theory, it failed to propose an alternative political vision to the monarchical models of traditional religion. Critics of patriarchal worship tended to propose either a garden or a simple utopian community. I was proposing a genuinely political alternative.

The Principles for Regeneration of Worship

What then, I had to ask, should be the principles by which we could go about re-building a political alternative to patriarchal monarchy? Here, I turned to the key concepts I had gathered together earlier around the notion of covenantal publicity, not only those of covenant and public, but also constitution, republic, and democracy. Such a constellation of symbols should deeply inform our language of worship. Within this symbolic framework, equality would exhibit not merely the notion of equal power, but the reality of participation in the life of our relevant publics. This included participation in the assembly (the *ekklesia*), of the church. The revitalization of congregational life, whether in Roman Catholic, Orthodox, or Protestant circles, was a key practical outcome. Along with the value of participation, the concept of personality would move from the concern for individual development and celebrity expression to engagement with actual publics focused on common tasks in a particular place. This was how I sought to recover the original meaning of persona as the way we present ourselves in public life.

From the perspective of covenantal publicity, the activity of governance, law, and constitution, rather than flowing from a unitary Godhead of authority and command, emerges within a field of discourse —the Logos in John's Gospel—that functions as the "Wisdom" of the body politic. This Wisdom can be understood in our own time through the cybernetic concepts of communication, feedback, constant re-equilibration, and comprehensive system awareness. This was a perspective that had emerged in my doctoral dissertation on body thinking in ecclesiology and cybernetics. Since then my symbolic awareness had been heightened by Sylvia's textile work on the tradition of Wisdom in biblical and spiritual thought. This was yet another connection between feminist thought and the political theory I was embedding in worship.

Very importantly, the concept of president as a religious symbol had to be placed within the notion of covenantal publicity. Presidency requires a participation in the constantly renewed wisdom of the public discourse. It is not the power of command as much as it is of ordering and guiding this discourse within the constitution of the republic. Even more important is an emphasis on "presiding" within this covenantal public rather than on the figure of a "president," who can very easily take on the monarchical traits of traditional kings and despots. In a little appendix to this book, I imagined a "conversation with President Jesus" that tried to explore the peculiar nature of his presidency and presiding spirit over against the conceptions that permeate our typical political life. It is only as I have tried to live into this imagery over the years, that I have come to a deeper appreciation of the symbol of Trinity as one that can address this dynamic, covenantal conception of presidency.

Some people, following arguments from the emperor Constantine to James I of England, thought that kingship best exemplified God's rule over the universe. Kings were "uncaused" rulers of their realm. They were above mere election by the people. However, in fact, kings were often elected or were simply victors in clan warfare. Election, which we associate with presidents, ought to be seen in the context of the mutual pledging of covenant binding a people together in a common calling. "Electing" God, far from being a self-contradiction, appealed to the God who enters into covenant with a people.

The rehearsal of this covenantal bond with God should be a central component of worship. In this worship we rehearse God's faithfulness, our rebellion and brokenness, and the healing work of forgiveness, reconciliation, and renewal. All of this propels worship to an eschatological outlook that lives in anticipation of the ultimate fulfilment of God's covenant with us to bring the creation to abundant life.

In short, participation in the worship assembly and the regular renewal of covenantal commitments should be central to worship. Moreover, to avoid the easy conflation of Christian worship with civil religion and, even worse, simple nationalism, worship had to preserve both its eschatological orientation and its commitment to the non-violent persuasion inherent in covenantal publicity. Our life in worship as in ethics is always an expression of the "not yet," of longing and aspiration. As part of this eschatological gap we must remember that the flow of symbols between church and general publics must emerge in a process of critical engagement, once again appealing to the values of reciprocal transformation in *Disciplines in Transformation*.

As a work of persuasion, worship rests on the testimonies embedded in ancient Scriptures as well as the slow work of acculturation through rituals and the recognition of the equality of every baptized citizen of the assembly. Each of these components appealed to critical elements of my own history in Evangelical and Calvinist Baptist churches and in Catholic priestly education. The importance of persuasion as a practice embedded in worship increasingly came to undergird my approach to reconciliation and peace-making, something that emerged in my work with greater prominence after this book.

Mindful of the motivational power of the links that had existed between worship and the world of patriarchy and kingship, I emphasized that any worship must have psychological depth. It must be able to connect people's inner needs, longings, and self-understandings to the symbols of God's wider order. Kingship had been able to draw on family symbols of father and household to ground its claim to authority and power. Worship in the universe of democratic and constitutional republics, however, had to draw on our inner drive for covenantal bonds and public life. The life of citizenship had to be rooted in the psychology of personal expression and public confirmation. Here I was working out the implications of my psychological approach in *God's Federal Republic* for the work of worship.

Since we enter into this public life as bodies, worship would also have to manifest "sensory holism." I was particularly mindful of the way much of Protestantism had been captured by an intellectual engagement with words. In going beyond that, however, it was not enough to give oneself over to the emotional ecstasy of enthusiastic revivals. That way lies the oppression of the charismatic demagogue. Sensory holism asks that the eye, ear, taste, touch, and smell be tied to the work of discourse in an assembly rich in intellectual as well as emotional traditions. Here, the analytical work I had done on the symbol of the Body of Christ in my dissertation moved into a more dramatic perspective grounded in worship practices.

Finally, effective worship requires what I called a "consistent grammar." If worship is first of all a drama, it cannot be simply a mélange of experiences unconnected without a plot. It has to have a consistent grammar. Like any public discourse, there has to be a logic, a wisdom, a narrative that holds it together so that it can be a genuine rehearsal of a script leading us on into a greater story.

Practical and Critical Ethical Considerations

I concluded these proposals with a fantasy about a worship practice that might exemplify these principles. It was characterized by circular process, efforts to re-present Scripture in worship, and greater participation within a structured liturgy and sermonic conversation. At its center was a round table to stress the equality of the citizens of the assembly. It was an image that would re-ignite my woodworking, in particular the round communion table I made for Andover Newton's chapel just before my retirement. I also tried to spell out how we might move from a church year focused on Advent-Christmas-Easter, with its emphasis on the birth, sacrifice, and victory of a king, to one that revolved around the work of the Holy Spirit celebrated at Pentecost. In addition, I introduced the question of how our worship drama could be better attuned to the ecological story of our natural year, if not of our universe. A dozen years later I would take up this question in work with one of my South African colleagues, Ernst Conradie, who has given major attention to this very question, especially in the context of a more robust eschatology.[8]

This effort to re-imagine worship led directly to many of the elements of the roundtable worship I introduced later to my congregation in North Carolina. The practices developed by Howard Hanger in the Jubilee! worship community in Asheville shaped some of these particulars as well, at least in their beginning. Others stretched back to our worship experiments in Atlanta and at Andover Newton.

Along with these matters of practice, there were also critical ethical questions to be addressed. The first, amplified by my experience in South Africa, asked whether a worship anchored in federal-republican and democratic visions was simply a limited ethno-centric replacement for the patriarchal monarchy of traditional worship. Was my proposal more a matter of culturally-bounded ethics than of theologically grounded worship? My

---

8. Among his extensive writings see Conradie, *Hope for the Earth*.

response, aside from the universal requirement for humility in all we propose, was to appeal not only to the values emerging from my understanding of our humanity itself but also to the primary work of peace-building. In a world rent with ethnic, religious, and military conflict, the patient commitment to council, persuasion, covenant, and public life still offers the best path to a peace that arises from agreement rather than domination.

The second question, part of my inherited prophetic tradition, was how to deal with the inevitable problem of idolatry. Is the generation of a vision of right governance in worship inevitably an idolization of a particular political ideology? Is it not better to remain in the diffuse images of mysticism or the natural Edens of the garden? For this prophetic critique I appealed once again to the need for an eschatological gap to attenuate our loyalties to any historical structure. But even more important, it seemed to me that the fundamental call to love and justice at the core of Christian (and Jewish and Muslim) heritage requires the struggle to articulate appropriate patterns of power and authority to pursue these ethical demands and visions. There is an inevitable, perhaps tragic, need to try to live out in actual institutional structures the intimations of justice and right order that emerge in our theological commitments. For this claim, like so many of my generation, I was indebted both to Reinhold Niebuhr, whose work permeated my college and graduate school years, and to Dietrich Bonhoeffer, who took on the work of resistance to Hitler's demonic tyranny. This effort to actually live into God's greater Republic, it seemed to me, requires the risky path I was proposing in this book. Its brevity should not conceal its importance in the development of my own thought and practice.

V

Beyond Prose

Wood and Word

THE INTENSIVE EXPLORATION OF the implications of my ethics of covenantal publicity for worship and the arts began to lead me back to my long interest in woodworking. As the century, indeed the millennium, neared its end, this interest became a tangible need to put my hands in play with actual material reality. I was already putting aside my academic journals to read *Fine Woodworking* as soon as it landed in my mailbox. I needed to balance the life of my mind with the work of my hands.

In the middle of a winter night in early 2000, I awoke with a distinct message in my mind which I later interpreted as arising from some Jungian archetype deep within me. "It's time," the voice said. "It's time to move on to a more balanced life." I decided to retire from my academic work and, in spite of the costs, return to western North Carolina. "Early," they said. "Just in time," said I. With that decision I began to envision making a round communion table for the chapel at Andover Newton to express the crystallization of my intellectual commitments in a tangible form that would shape the life of worship. Constructing the table would somehow be the first act of this new phase of my life.

During our years at Andover Newton we returned to our home in the Great Smoky Mountains each summer and Christmas holiday. That summer I took local cherry, maple, holly, and walnut and put together a round, double gateleg dropleaf table. Sylvia made a mosaic center for it depicting the descent of the Pentecostal dove. Wood inlays of a dogwood-flower cross within a mandorla and of a shell within the classic circles of the Trinity to symbolize baptism completed the ornamentation. The double gatelegs, in my mind, symbolized both the gates of the ancient city where judgment was declared as well as the doorways of entry into a new life.

One of my doctoral students, Mary Macrina Cowan, suggested I keep a journal of this experience, which I drew from for an article in *The Christian Century* in 2001 about the meaning of constructing the table. In it, I reflected on how deeply the image of the roundtable experience in the old East Germany as well as the combination of Protestant Word and Catholic Eucharist had worked their way into my hands as I cut, planed, sanded, and joined wood from the trees that surrounded me in the Appalachian forests. It would not be a table set opposite the pulpit, it would be a table where "word and table" became "word at table." It would be a place of conversation as well as nurture.

Construction of the table in 2000 became the symbol of a turning point in my life. My mother, who had been the source of so much of my mystical emotion and spirituality (not to mention my excessive moralism) had died in May of 1999. Then, even as I was delivering the Commencement Address at Andover Newton in May of 2001, my father died, his life of faithful stewardship and self-effacing good cheer concluded. I was at the head of the line now and needed to move into new territory according to my own lights.

The Roundtable Project: Worship and the Work of Reconciliation

STRETCHING BACK TO MY earliest years conducting those little Christmas Eve services, I had been drawn to the dynamics of worship in small groups. In the last fifteen years of the century this attraction gradually took the form of the circular worship of conversation and nurture embodied in the round communion table. In the late 1980s Sylvia and I had led such a small worship group to experiment with these emerging ideas in Atlanta. Now this impulse returned with much broader foundations and elaboration.

In the last couple of years at Andover Newton I got into conversation with Tom Porter, a United Methodist minister and lawyer, who had turned to developing processes of mediation and conflict resolution as an expression of the work of reconciliation. The practices of circle conversation developed largely in Native American and Canadian First Nation traditions lay at the center of this work. Instead of seeking retribution and punishment, these circles sought a justice of restoration and healing. Tom had helped found a ministry within the United Methodist Church called JustPeace in order to express this vision and develop its practices.

As we talked about this model it became clear that the circle conversation at a round table was the proper way to embody this process in worship, where it could deepen and enlarge our sense of justice and grace. He soon asked me to build a round communion table for his church in Wellesley, Massachusetts, that could be used in JustPeace worship. I completed it in 2004, taking it to Nashville, Tennessee, for use in a JustPeace Conference. Over the next ten years I built two tables for my church in Waynesville, North Carolina, as well as tables for the Baltimore-Washington Conference, for Boston University School of Theology, and several others. In each of them, I was not only developing my theory of worship but also honing my skills as a woodworker. The values of patience, care, ecological awareness, and self-discipline were also integral to the values embedded in the way I came to understand the work of reconciliation.

My intuitive attraction to worship in circle, shared with many other people, now had a theological home in the concepts of reconciliation and covenantal publicity that I had worked out in *God's Federal Republic* and *Praying for God's Republic*. I began to develop these ideas with a series of articles, starting with a piece for the journal *Faith and Form*.[1] Here, I recounted our visit in 1998 to the unusual circular domed church in the countryside north of Durban, South Africa, in Kwa-Zulu Natal.

For many years Sylvia had kept an issue of *Time* magazine with a picture of this exquisite church, hoping we might someday have the chance to visit it. Fr. Anton Maier, a German priest who had worked for decades among the Zulu people, had constructed this unusual church in the village of Nchingabantu to draw on the traditions of a Zulu king's ceremonial dwelling. We met Fr. Maier at the crossroads of Seven Oaks and set out to follow him over dusty and increasingly narrow roads, stopping occasionally as he chatted with parishioners or gave them a ride. We finally stopped and climbed over a hill among grazing cattle in late afternoon fog and approached the large domed structure we had known only on the wrinkled page of the magazine.

1. Everett, "Finding the Ethics."

Making My Way in Ethics, Worship, and Wood

He took us through the low doorway and past a Zulu madonna flanked by a warrior-like Zulu Jesus and entered into its circular room to behold a sanctuary deeply shaped by its environing Zulu culture. It was an unforgettable holy experience. Its striking construction and imaginative engagement with both traditional and contemporary symbols enabled me to reflect in a vivid way on the difficult challenge of moving between the inherited traditions of patriarchal monarchy and the ideals of democratic citizenship seeking to find root in South Africa's post-apartheid world.

It also challenged me to think in terms of the way architecture shapes our relationships, our memory, our vision for the future, and our conception of our place in the universe. How we are situated in space is a crucial element in the symbolic universe in which we map our life's journey. As someone who had never excelled in dance and sportive movement, this required opening up my senses in a different way that I now see as very important to our spiritual life as well as our ecological understanding. A church building needs not only to be ecologically green but also to form us in the relationships that reflect our understanding of God's right order. Church buildings are not merely functional spaces for group activities. They are also expressions of faith in themselves. This awareness was now reinforcing my desire to create appropriate church furniture to reflect this symbolic world.

Through symposiums put together by Tom Porter and Professor Howard Vogel at Hamline School of Law in St. Paul, Minnesota, I was able to work out more thoroughly the way ritual, including movement and symbols, was foundational to the process of circle conversation and reconciliation. For one of those symposiums I reflected on the ways ritual and symbols underpin and give authoritative form to the search for restorative justice through circle processes. In an article entitled "Ritual Wisdom and Restorative Justice," I pointed out how "ritual and symbols exercise their peculiar social power in at least three ways: by legitimating action, by ordering relationships, and by enabling people to 'rehearse' their participation in the resolution of conflict."[2]

Here I appealed once again to the dramatic character of worship and to the way powerful religious symbols authorize particular ways of seeking justice and restoration. Addressing the architecture of courtrooms, I pointed out the significance of shifts from the hierarchy of elevated seats and adversarial positions to the circular authority of engaging all the stakeholders

---

2. Everett, "Ritual Wisdom," 349.

in a conflict in the search for appropriate ways to hold offenders accountable and repair the damage they have caused. A judicial proceeding is not just a science-like effort to find the "truth" and make judgments. It is a drama appealing to basic cultural convictions that provide legitimacy to its work of judging injury and repairing harm.

Worship is also a peculiar drama inviting worshippers into a great story that gives meaning to their lives. In working out my understanding of these dramatic forms, I returned to the concept of persona that I had worked with thirty years earlier and which has constantly recurred to me as I tried to express the crucial passage from private to public life. In a drama we gain a "personhood"—a role by which to enter into the interaction as witness, as offender, as victim, as agent of reconciliation, and as judge. To participate in these dramas, one has to become or take on a persona. With regard to wider reality, there is no self without the persona. Calls to take away our public masks (the original meaning of persona) destroy our capacity to live into relationships, whether of justice or of love. The construction of these personae is not a dissimulation of our "real self" but the way we become actors in the construction of a more just and mutually confirming world. Central to law as well as worship is a concept of the self that is a person rather than a scientist or an economic utilitarian. Though I had never gotten very involved in theater, these convictions gave me a deep appreciation of its contribution to our personal as well as public life.

In 2005 Tom Porter brought a number of people together to assemble a book of essays linking the work of conflict transformation to the act of "coming to the table" in worship. He called it *Conflict and Communion: Reconciliation and Restorative Justice at Christ's Table*. In my own essay[3] I lifted up the practices that were emerging in the roundtable worship at my church in Waynesville. I pointed out that gathering at table in a circle contrasts with our inherited traditions of facing an altar of sacrifice. Sacrificial paradigms place us in a hierarchical relation with an ultimate authority to which sacrifices are offered. The offering of the Son to the Father has been central to most Christian worship and theology. It is a kind of pyramid of sacrifice. The circle, however, engages us with the work of the Holy Spirit that enables us to listen and speak to one another in searching for God's purpose for our lives.

"The roundtable," I wrote, "sees reconciliation as a new relationship among women and men who have been baptized into the equality of a new

---

3. Everett, "Gathering at the Roundtable."

assembly. While the altar focuses on obedience, the table lifts up persuasion, mutual empathy, and the dynamics of circle process…" Worship of this kind, I concluded, "is an energizing source, a grounding of our lives in the historical drama of reconciliation that takes place in specific contexts in a language of the place and people in conflict. The work of conflict transformation in specific situations stands at the heart of what the reconciliation rehearsed in worship is all about."

This reflection then led me to work with regular participants in the roundtable worship gathering at our church to lay out more fully the theological and practical dimensions of what we were doing. Our roundtable worship began in the midst of our despair and hope as our country embarked on a devastating and ill-conceived invasion of Iraq in the winter of 2003. While there were many other conflicts tearing the fabric of our communities apart, this is the one that galvanized our gathering in conversation, prayer, and song.

The simple table I built of maple and walnut for our gatherings displayed at its center two crossed mandorlas with a small sphere of purpleheart wood to symbolize that indeed there is still a heart of sacrifice and self-giving in the midst of the intersecting circles of the two mandorlas. By extending the arcs of the circles beyond the fish-shaped "*vesica pisces*" that constitutes the classic mandorla, I tried to indicate that the circle reaches out beyond the table to bring in those beyond the group assembled for its nurture and conversation. The pedestal also consisted of circular shapes to reinforce this dynamic of inclusion.

In this essay I emphasized that Christ's Spirit "presides" at the table. By emphasizing the verb "preside," I tried to get beyond the static notion of president that could so easily take on the monarchical authority of classical theology. Moreover, this presidency of the Spirit connected with the Wisdom tradition in Scripture as well as many features of democratic consensus-building.

To shape the presidency of Christ's Spirit at the table, we use a Cherokee talking piece consisting of a turkey feather in a leather handle. Its lightness helps convey the ineffable spirit of honest, heart-felt communication and deep listening at the heart of circle conversation. This does not preclude the use of other talking pieces, but is emblematic of the spirit we seek to invoke in our gatherings.

I then laid out the somewhat classic components of Christian worship that shape our gathering: the Call to the Table, the Invocation and

Confirmation of God's Presence (through the lighting of a candle), the Remembrance of the tradition in which we stand, and the Thanksgiving for what is present at table, leading to the sharing of something to eat and drink, usually based on the fruit of the grape and the wheat-based bread. This leads into a reading to focus our thoughts and prepare us for the conversation concerning a particularly important matter relevant to our community. This is followed by a time of prayer as we extend the conversation into our ultimate dialogue with God and the wider assemblies throughout the world gathered in God's spirit. We conclude with a contemporary rendering of Jesus's prayer form in Matthew and Luke, which we call the "Hope Prayer," and a recitation of our key commitments around reconciliation and peace. At this point, we have used this basic form for over fifteen years.

Roundtable Worship and Peace-Building

This work on liturgy and restorative justice spilled over into working with Sylvia to provide artistic installations and liturgies for the Lake Junaluska Peace Conference at nearby Lake Junaluska Conference Center, which began in 2008. After the first conference I encouraged the planning committee to conceive of it as an interfaith conference among the three Abrahamic religions: Judaism, Christianity, and Islam. It thus became the Lake Junaluska Interfaith Peace Conference. While peace-building as a theme was always a natural player in my mind, it was usually as an outcome of the work of deepening the political vision of federal, democratic republicanism. Working with the Peace Conference over the ensuing years helped me flesh out this dimension of my work.

Over the years I had been in conversation with Glen Stassen, whom I had known since my years as a teenager in Washington. Doctoral work at Union Theological Seminary in New York had led him into an academic career in Christian ethics. Glen had worked out a framework for connecting biblical themes of peace to specific practices of peace-building. In 1977 he invited me to spend a semester at Berea College as a guest professor. Aside from my summer at Philander Smith College, it was my only experience of undergraduate teaching until a semester at the University of Cape Town in my retirement. My semester at Berea inspired a long-term interest in the school's work, including its dedication to the rich craft traditions of this region. Glen's work informed my subsequent involvement with the Lake Junaluska Interfaith Peace Conference, where I continued to fill out some of the implications of my own conception of the relation of worship and the arts to the work of peace.

I was also stimulated by the ongoing attention given to this connection of worship and peace by Ken Sehested, founder of the Baptist Peace Fellowship of North America. We had gotten to know Ken, and his wife Nancy, one of the first women ordained for ministry in a Southern Baptist church, when they came to Lake Junaluska and stayed in our house in nearby Waynesville for one harsh winter while they were re-locating. With their colleague Joyce Hollyday, they founded a congregation in Asheville that incorporated circular motifs and commitments along the lines we were developing in roundtable worship. I believe that this form of worship and spiritual formation will continue to provide a norm for worship life in many places and cultures in coming years.

With my retirement, the long gestation of these themes in the dialogue of worship and ethics, leading to the focus on restorative justice and reconciliation, began to effect a change in my writing pursuits. Along with woodworking, I began to think about engaging in a narrative project that would bring together my South Africa experience, my deepening awareness of Cherokee culture around us in the southern Appalachians, my ecological commitments, and my understanding of reconciliation. It also began the turn to incorporating my own history, along with Sylvia's, into my own personal narrative as well as my writing.

Red Clay, Blood River: Reconciliation, Ecology, and Narrative

My passage from the abstract world of ethics and theology to the narrative world of an historical novel was as important as that from writing to woodworking. In both cases, it was a movement toward the concrete, the tangible, the historically and geographically bound particular. As I immersed myself in this story, I left behind the grid of conceptual boxes and entered the linear succession of unrepeatable specifics that constitutes history. As Max Weber, whose work had shaped me earlier, wrote at the beginning of the twentieth century, I was moving from the "nomothetic" world of rules to the "ideographic" world of persons and events.

But this move was not unprepared for by earlier events in my life. At Wesleyan University I had started out with a keen interest in mathematics, only to realize that I felt unmoored by the loss of any concrete references for the symbols of a multitude of abstract and formal equations. I soon moved, with the creation of Wesleyan's College of Social Studies, into the historical world of ethics, politics, and history, with a dose of economic theory to satisfy my lingering mathematical thirst. By the time I reached my sixties, the geometry and calculations of woodworking would satisfy my mathematical instincts, along with occasional absorption in pictures from the Hubble telescope.

More importantly, my divorce and re-marriage in the early 1980s tore me out of my life-long effort to act according to abstract ethical values like duty, covenant, honesty, fidelity, and forgiveness and thrust me into the specific decisions we finite individuals have to make in the midst of conflicting loyalties, commitments, habits, and loves. Life was not so much a matter of being "good" or "better" but of forming a coherent and faithful story of grace and redemption out of our actual capacities, needs, hopes, and longings. Hundreds of pages of journal writings as well as a personal novel emerged as I struggled to envision these transformative chapters of my life, chapters that I had never dreamed I would have to create. My deep commitment to a covenantal understanding of life meant that I had to enter the history of making, breaking, and renewing covenant that this faith requires. Life was less the movement toward perfection that John Wesley had lifted up, and more a journey with the Lover of our lives. But even then, it was less a movement toward a goal than it was the story of relationships, of fragile hopes, brokenness, forgiveness, and healing. It was a story not only of a journey but also of an ever-richer struggle with time, body, earth, and space. The experiences arising in my own life began, over twenty years later, to shape the writing of a larger saga connecting many aspects of my public life and commitments.

Soon after leaving Andover Newton I began to collect and sift information for a novel that was emerging out of many strands from my own history as well as Sylvia's. The twisted skeins of history were manifold indeed. I began with the genealogical work Sylvia had done in the 1980s when we moved to Atlanta, Georgia. Her ancestry, she found, included a line through her mother that went back to a man named Valentin Thrash, who came from Germany in 1740. Valentin, who, we discovered, was buried near our home in North Carolina, fought in the Rutherford expedition in western North Carolina that set out in 1776 to wipe out, with terrible cruelty, the villages of the Cherokee who were siding with the British against the land-hungry colonists. His route passed directly beneath our mountainside retirement home in the Smokies.

His brother, it seems, had emigrated to Yorkshire, England. One of his descendants went to South Africa. Another side of her ancestry included a woman, Tabitha Bagwell, who the family said had been Cherokee. We had a picture of her daughter Zenobia holding ears of corn at her wedding that seemed to corroborate this story. Indeed, a later DNA test showed Sylvia with eleven percent Native American ancestry.

The South Africa connection intrigued me and became the stem on which I constructed a narrative leading up to the "Great Trek" of emigrant Dutch farmers who left English-controlled South Africa to seize land from the Zulus and others in order to continue their Afrikaner way of life. This was not the only connection between Africa and America, for I soon discovered, upon settling near Cherokee, North Carolina, that some of the nineteenth century Cherokees had been slaveholders, just as the white farmers they sought to emulate and compete with. This was part of their becoming a "civilized" nation with their own form of writing, laws, and increasingly European and colonial customs.

This led me to burrow into the increasingly voluminous knowledge of the slave trade that has accumulated at the Dubois Institute at Harvard University and elsewhere. It was possible to trace a slave ship and its captives from Mozambique to Cape Town and then to the Americas, where a well-to-do Cherokee could have purchased slaves coming in through the port of Charleston, South Carolina. Indeed, there were numerous enslaved Africans on the Trail of Tears whose descendants are still living in Oklahoma.

Moreover, I discovered that the American Board of Foreign Missions, established at Andover Theological School in the nineteenth century, had sent missionaries both to the Cherokee, where they played a major role in developing Cherokee culture and defending them from attack, and also to South Africa. One of them, Daniel Lindley, accompanied the Afrikaners on their way to defeat Zulu forces on the Ncome River in the same month of 1838 as the displaced Cherokee on the Trail of Tears confronted the challenge of crossing the ice-jammed Mississippi River.

On the way, I unearthed the involvement of two of my collateral ancestors in this American tragedy: Edward Everett, an ardent opponent of Cherokee removal, and his brother Alexander Hill Everett, who was a State Department witness to the spurious Treaty of New Echota (1835) that began the removal of the Cherokee from their ancestral lands. Though they did not make it into my book, their presence intensified my connection to its story.

The warp for a saga exploring the intricacies of our histories and their connections across oceans was now strung into place. I began weaving in the actions of both fictional and historical figures to tell my story. People began to show up, even in my dreams. Marietjie (Marie) Tillman, a young woman from South Africa, was soon joined by Clayton Bagwell, a Cherokee from Oklahoma, and Lanier Johnson, an African-American from Atlanta. All three came together as students at the Institute of Ecology at the University of Georgia, a tableau that anchored the ecological thrust of the narrative.

In Africa a woman named Thembinkosi ("trust in the Lord") becomes the bearer of the African connection as she is seized in Mozambique, taken to Cape Town as a slave, and, after the brutal death of her lover, is taken to Charleston while bearing his child, where she is sold to Valentin Thrash. Her story leads all the way to Lanier Johnson, one of the ecology students who form a foil and point of interrogation for the whole novel.

In the story, Valentin himself, after being part of the devastating Rutherford raid on the Cherokees, eventually marries a young Cherokee woman. Her name is Tabitha, the name of Sylvia's Cherokee ancestor. Such marriages, far from being rare, occurred throughout pioneer times.

The connection of the Thrash family to South Africa was verified by our visit to a Thrash descendant's grave in Pietermaritzburg. In order to sense the geography and history of the Great Trek, we took two trips across South Africa from Cape Town, travelling the historical routes through the Eastern Cape to Blood River in present-day Kwa-Zulu Natal. Out of this rich historical background the figures of Grace and her Afrikaner husband Fortius emerged to bear the tale of the Great Trek.

To begin to weave all these strands together, I employed two conventions of fiction writing. One was to focus on a mirrored compact, acquired in exchange for ivory by Thembinkosi's father. Broken in two by her captors, one half of the compact accompanies Thembinkosi through her incredible journey, ending on the Trail of Tears. Its eventual reunion with its other half is one of the key symbols of human interconnection as well as reconciliation across all historical and biological divisions. The meaning of the word "compact" as an aid for personal beautification and also as a covenantal agreement linked two sides of my own development in ethics and aesthetics. In this case the compact, like ancient biblical covenant, was a public bond of memory, faithfulness, and hope that constituted Thembinkosi's history.

The other convention was even more ambitious. It was to turn to Earth as the narrator of these events. This meant that the widespread point of view of the omniscient third-person narrator in most fiction ("he thought," "she felt," etc.) were set aside. I had always found them epistemologically problematic. Earth could only tell of the impact of voices, bodies, and objects that reach her bodily surface (where is that personal, non-gendered pronoun?). Only Earth could know of the otherwise unremarked connections that my protagonists were enmeshed in across time and space. It was a way of taking an ecological point of view on human history. This decision demanded that I enter into the actual drama of their history in a way that reframes what history is. It demanded that history be understood as eco-history. Moreover, because Earth cannot know what is going on in our minds, the narrative took on the shape of a drama built around the dialogue and actions of the principals. This move to dramatic dialogue was reflected in my turn from the didactic message of preaching to the drama of reconciliation as the true heart of worship. The conversation at table in search of God's graceful healing had already replaced the traditional sermon. Now it was shaping this saga of ecological reconciliation.

This knitting together of ecology and history shaped the title of the book. Red Clay is the site in north Georgia of the Cherokee council that set in motion their passage toward removal on the Trail of Tears. Blood River referred to the bloody battle on the Ncome River in Kwa-Zulu Natal that marked the Afrikaners' seizing of Zulu land at the culmination of their trek out of British colonial Africa. Both became emblems of victory as well as defeat. Themes of clay, river, blood, and beauty thread their way through the whole narrative.

I discovered that the fictional world novelists create can easily become their seemingly real world as they dream of conversations among their characters or work through emotional crises in their life. When I told one of my friends in ethics that I was working on a piece of fiction, he quickly replied, "But, Bill, you've always been writing fiction!" While he was right about the way the high ideals guiding my work in ethics always bore a good deal of immediate impracticality, he did not see what a marked turn this was in the way I approached the struggle of human beings to act into a life and a world beyond their narrow egoism.

Beyond Prose

The narrative of *Red Clay, Blood River* sought to confront both the enormous conflicts among humans and also those between humanity and the earth. It was a way to re-conceive the work of reconciliation within a narrative framework. It was also a way to think about the meaning of ecological as well as human and spiritual reconciliation. The tiny fragment of Earth's memory constructed out of Sylvia's and my own family histories was simply a reflection of this wider work of creative reconciliation.

In placing the historically grounded work of reconciliation in a wider ecological framework, *Red Clay, Blood River* was also reaching back to the themes I first raised in my article on land ethics in 1979. However, rather than arising in a grid of interlocking claims and concepts, these concerns took a narrative form that left much more room for ambiguity, incompleteness, and, yes, tragedy. But this new construction was not merely evidence of the hard-won wisdom of an aging life, it was also an expansion of perspective that was resonating with a growing ecological consciousness in the industrialized as well as "developing" world.

Red Clay, Blood River not only expanded the range of my ethical palette. It also brought to the surface the poetic expression that had arisen in the anguish and ecstasy of my passage through divorce and into a new marriage. The explosion of poetry by which I sought to grasp what was happening in my life at that time re-emerged in new form to shape each sentence of a novel about our common struggle for a renewed covenant with the world itself. The world of prose—administrative, academic, legal, and didactic—that enveloped me until my retirement had kept a tight lid on poetic expression, but now it began to emerge with a robust flowering.

Red Clay, Blood River begins with an "ecologue" by Earth that sets the geological and historical context for the human story to follow. The cadence, word choice, and even rhyme that characterize the narrative give evidence that it arose as a spoken dialogue in my mind. The conviction that poetry is first of all to be spoken, indeed performed, continues to shape how I put words on a page for the eye. For me, poetry remains, as it was for Homer, primarily a casting of words to speak and sing. The discipline of speaking through Earth's perceptions made me focus on descriptive words that cling to the rocks, plants, water, sounds, and smells that shape our sense of who and where we are in the physical world. The words had body. The body thinking of my dissertation had become "body speaking," expressions of the tangible materials of earth's body, of our bodies.

Making My Way in Ethics, Worship, and Wood

Turning from Prose to Poetry and Song

The poetry that emerged in the 1980s began to find expression in hymns and songs as I turned to developing practices of worship in the 1990s. Although my musical training was largely restricted to what I had picked up in choral singing and folk guitar, melodies began to show up in my mind. Words began to spill out to ride the notes. The guitar I had been playing since the sixties began to help me shape some music that would join the movement toward a worship centered at the table of reconciliation. Strains in my writing began to find resonance with the worship forms that had been developing over the years. Indeed, it was only by writing new songs that I could begin to experiment with the use of the language of *God's Federal Republic* in a medium usually dominated by medieval and monarchical symbolism.

When we had settled into our year-round life in North Carolina, I began to attend poetry and writing workshops and conferences, as well as take up conversation with local poets and writers. While I was not a "regional Appalachian writer," I began to appreciate more deeply our local writers' care for language, for its sound, and for its connection to place and purpose. Of singular importance in encouraging me to give voice to my poetry was Kathryn Stripling Byer, who said with delight that "nobody writes poetry like that any more." But rather than seeing me simply as a throwback, she, along with her colleague Newton Smith, helped me find my own lyric voice, which led to publication of a set of poems in a volume I called *Turnings: Poems of Transformation*. Kay was North Carolina's first woman Poet Laureate, and she worked tirelessly to promote the art and craft of poetry. With many others, I was deeply saddened by her untimely death in 2017.

I used the words turning and transformation in the title, because poetry was for me a means for my own inner transformation, just as I see transformation going on all around me. These transformations also call for the kind of turning in our life course connected with religious conversion. The connection to the turning of wood, of course, was also not far from my mind. Life is not merely change, but, from a theological standpoint, transformation, a longing for the greater creativity and beauty contained in the original creation of the universe and of our own lives. Aside from the conventions of cadence and spoken form, this is another reason why poetry for me claps hands with liturgy and worship.

While not formally educated in poetry and literature, I can see some of the discipline's streams that feed into my writing. In my poetry I see the playfulness with words inspired by e. e. cummings (whose Latin teacher in Cambridge, Cecil Derry, also helped me with my Latin) and the music of Charles Ives. My care for cadence arises not only from the classical language of the English Bible, but also the hymns that I have sung my whole life. My celebration of the sheer extravagance of sounds in English as well as of the religious depth of experience has clearly been fed by Gerard Manley Hopkins. The structural form of my poems frequently follows the logical mold of the outline patterns of my books and essays. Line breaks are governed by my desire to instruct the reader in how to speak the lines out loud. They are designed for the voice rather than the eye.

This commitment to the voicing of words is clearly related to my concern for public speech. While I don't assume we can go back to the oratory of an Edward Everett, I find our current inability to cultivate clear and compelling public speech to be part of the lamented decay of public life and the formal publics of government, university, and church. Part of this erosion of civility is due to the tidal wave of trivial media interruptions of our daily life. A good deal of it is part of the decline in public reason, argument, and rational persuasion before the onslaught of marketed impulse. In this respect, my journey deeper into poetry was another expression of the commitments to publicity and covenanted relationships that arose in my academic writing.

Poetry further intensified my economy of words, a tendency that may have often made my earlier writings too dense and cryptic for many readers. But in poetry I could pursue, with different intent, the pruning of excess verbiage that usually hides more than it reveals the essential truth we are trying to express. Poetry, for me, should exhibit a humble economy of words as well as their creative exploitation.

The themes of my poems ranged widely from ecstatic love poems to elegies, laments, and shouts of praise before the awesome wonder of the universe. In times of inner turmoil, pain, or sorrow, they were fiery tapers leading me back to the light. In times of joy, they helped me seize and remember life's moments of transcendence. In them, black holes and galaxies figure as much as elephants, ants, and children. Irony often laces my poems on politics and warfare, joining an outraged moral sense with the awareness of our own fallibility. And some poems simply end with a warm smile. Poetic enunciation was the lens through which I came to see wide stretches of the world in my experience, whether in South Africa, New Mexico, Cyprus, or my Appalachian home.

The monthly roundtable worship liturgies as well as regular liturgical elements in our church's worship and the Interfaith Peace Conference have steadily accommodated my poetic work. Liturgical cadence and public speech have informed my poetry just as my poetry has sought to open up worship beyond the dry prose that infects the liturgy of our churches. Sometimes, I think the worship materials I am asked to read in worship were written by a committee of lawyers rather than someone inspired by the Spirit of God. While there is always the danger that my liturgical poetry will simply become obscure or idiosyncratic, I try to remain intent on concrete metaphors of the senses and the physical world as I open up our common voice to more transcendent realities.

This life-long confluence of worship, poetry, ethics, theology, public life, and, yes, woodworking always raises the question of whether I should have taken on the role of pastor rather than teacher; that is, whether my host institution and role definition should have been ecclesiastical rather than academic. While there are many reasons for my taking one institutional road rather than the other, it may finally boil down to the way in which I could not honestly speak the traditional words of church worship nor could my mind and imagination find adequate expression in the church roles I knew in my younger years. That I have exercised leadership, even a kind of pastoral leadership, in churches over the years has always arisen in the tension between my own imaginative and intellectual world and the constraints of inherited roles. This discomfort within institutions, especially large institutions, also abraded against my work in academic and seminary life. In my fifties it gradually sapped my energy for academic life, leading me to retire from my professorial role to devote myself to the constellation of work that I have pursued in the last twenty years. I have studied the life of institutions but my own temperament has not suited me well for working and thriving within them. Perhaps, as some say, we always study what we can't master, seeking another form of mastery than the immediately practical.

This tension in my personality and intellect came to greater self-consciousness as I committed myself to working with wood, whether in worship furnishings or simply in bowls, tables, and cabinets. There I discovered what Hannah Arendt had named much earlier, in *The Human Condition*, as the difference between work and action, between the maker and the actor.

In the peculiar making of worship furniture I was also acting into the ritual dramas that shape many people's lives.

Sawdust and Soul

The round communion table that formed the bridge from my academic career to one more engaged with creative material expression soon led to a number of other woodworking projects. In going to South Africa in 1998 I discovered that John de Gruchy had also turned to a long-neglected woodworking enthusiasm to balance his academic work. For his retirement symposium in Cape Town in 2003, I reflected on the meaning of this craft commitment in a little article entitled "With the Grain: Woodworking, Spirituality, and the Struggle for Justice," which was later published in *The Journal of Theology for Southern Africa*. I am sure some of the participants in that academic gathering were rather perplexed to find themselves facing an array of John's bowls and carvings as part of their celebration of his intellectual accomplishments!

In that essay I explored the way the ethical values of such craft work—patience, honest dialogue with the materials, collaboration, self-discipline, humility, and the like—were embedded in many of the virtues Jesus appealed to in his teachings as well as in the monastic and sectarian movements of later centuries. Many Christian virtues can be seen as the expression of an artisan craft ethic. This had fueled much of Christianity's ambivalence about public life, with its appeal to appearance, self-advancement, and the ephemera of opinion and memory. The values of honest workmanship and artisan excellence led craftspeople to communal, socialist or "small-is-beautiful" visions of the good life that were imperiled by the machinery of mass-production, capitalism, and globalization. The appeals of the prophets to the agrarian ideals of ancient Israel were harmonious with this artisan ethic. Joseph, as we all like to point out, was a *tekton*, a builder, which the forest-dwelling Christians of Europe translated to carpenter.

These craft values certainly resonated with what I had been discovering about myself as I moved away from my academic period. I came to acknowledge more deeply how the agrarian world of my family's farm, at least as I experienced it as a boy, played at least as large a role in my psyche as the public life of Washington that had guided much of my career. In the language of the OIKOS Project, I had lived a long time in the open and even fragmented oikos of my urban and mobile life, but my core image was a much tighter oikos of a town characterized by deeper interpersonal relationships and attention to the craft values of honesty, integrity, and workmanship. And, indeed, my retirement years have been a discovery and appreciation of these rural and town values in the remarkable community where we live in the southern Appalachians. Here, the artisan values of craftsmanship intersect with the life of a face-to-face public along the ancient ideals of the Greek city–state where the core of our political theory began. That it also lies in the fault line between plantation slavery and mountaineer isolation is part of the trauma we have yet to heal.

My turn to woodworking in this environment was not merely a mental matter. It was a physical matter of needing to work with my hands in order to feel balanced, integral, and whole. It was visceral. It was spiritual. In some sense my workshop became a chapel of my spirit, what Sylvia came to call my "woodchurch."

My numerous trips to South Africa, as well as John's trips to the US, further deepened this common appreciation of the role of woodworking in our lives. We decided to collaborate on a book of conversations about woodworking and spirituality that emerged in 2015 as *Sawdust and Soul*. These reflections on one of humanity's oldest crafts were facilitated enormously by the communication revolution that enabled us to trade pictures and texts on a daily basis, an irony that did not escape us as we attended to the deep personal and spiritual satisfactions of the work of hand and wood.

Along with observations about the meaning of woodworking for our spiritual and communal life, I was also able to see how cabinet-making recalled the boxes and grids in which I had sorted out intellectual concepts in my earlier career. Fitting tenon and mortise, drawer and carcass, panel and rabbet exercised a satisfaction to eye and hand, just as my careful delineations of patterns of Christianity, society, and personality had shaped my academic work thirty years earlier. Finding the exact fit of parts and then planning out the sequence of assembly reflected the intellectual task I had performed in books, articles, and lectures over the years.

With John's encouragement, I took up work on a lathe. With woodturning, I could move into a more linear narrative. If cabinetry reflected my academic work, woodturning reflected the irreversible line of narrative that emerged in my historical novel. Poetry itself employs both dynamics, as I assemble and reassemble its individual lines and words to create the verbal flow that best expresses the underlying image empowering the poem. As curls spun off from the wood, I was drawn to the flow of a line rather than the fine fit of pieces in a work of joinery. The roundness of my tables became the essence of the forms emerging on the lathe.

Living within one of the world's great hardwood forests, I was in a paradise for woodworkers and craftspeople. This has deepened the innate bond I have always felt with trees. I even gave a sermon as a student at Yale Divinity School that was simply a conversation with the pine tree outside the windows of Marquand Chapel! Trees continue to stand at the pivot among my interests in religion (check out Genesis 2 and Revelation 22), ecology, woodworking, and my own spirit. While my last breath will probably not be among these particular trees around our home, I hope it is in the spread of this ancient arboreal mountain range.

This ecological integrity is not, however, the whole skein of my life. Just as *Red Clay, Blood River* reflected the deep fissure between earth and its warring inhabitants, so there were other strands in my heritage I still had not recognized and struggled with. Even before John and I put *Sawdust and Soul* together, Sylvia had suggested that we spend our thirtieth anniversary looking for my grandfather Jackson's mine on Cyprus. I had no idea what door this trip would open in my memory and my life.

Mining Memories and the Work of Reconciliation

Red Clay, Blood River had drawn on Sylvia's ancestors and other sources to construct a fictional narrative that expanded my concepts of ecological awareness, human reconciliation, and global citizenship. In it the political visions of *God's Federal Republic* expanded into an ecological framework and the work of reconciliation shouldered a more complex and multi-layered meaning. This narrative work also was a way to live into the heritage I had adopted when Sylvia and I came together and I took her family name for my middle name.

Sylvia's suggestion to find the copper mine where my maternal grandfather had worked and where my mother and her family had lived in the 1920s opened up yet another avenue for re-appropriating my past and examining earth from another perspective. This past had always been present in my life through a collection of glass and ceramic antiquities that I had inherited from my grandparents. They had brought back Roman lamps from the first century CE that had been dug up in the ancient mine as well as vases and tear bottles stretching back another millennium. Yet I knew little of the history surrounding their acquisition. My mother's father, who died when I was only four, was a mining engineer from Minnesota, whose Mesabi iron ore ranges gave him his first experience in the world of immigrant labor, heavy machinery, and the often dangerous implementation of mining technology. He then went to Arizona's copper region, where, my mother told me, the "Wobblies" (International Workers of the World) had a contract out on him, because of his close association with the mine owners. He slept with a pistol under his pillow, so the story went, and told my grandmother to wake him if she got up in the night, lest he mistakenly shoot her as an intruder. He was a pious man with a fierce temper, who threatened to move to Canada when FDR won his third (and fourth) term. His sudden death from a cerebral hemorrhage in Toronto in 1945 meant that he was only a faint image in my memory, though closer to my psyche than I ever knew.

It was in Arizona that representatives of the newly formed Cyprus Mines Corporation approached him about going to the recently re-discovered ancient copper mine in Skouriotissa, Cyprus.[4] I had grown up with stories and artifacts of their two-year stay at an old monastery compound there, but I didn't know where the mine was or really what had happened during their two-year sojourn. What I found opened new doors into my memory, my past, and a world conjoined to my central interests in ecology, federalism, restorative justice, and reconciliation.

My sister Lois began to unearth some of their photographs and papers that had been stashed in an old cabinet at our family home in Virginia. With a small album of some of these photos we set off to Cyprus in 2012. The story not only of their experiences on Cyprus but of our adventure of exploration to recover them eventually resulted in a book, *Mining Memories on Cyprus, 1923-1925*. In the process I discovered not only the power of digital technology for rehabilitating the pictures my grandmother had developed and processed while on Cyprus but also the power of these photographs to evoke a relationship with the people and places of that storied island.

Immersion in my grandfather's world, both historically and contemporaneously, helped me discover elements of character, cultural values, and even physiognomy that I had not acknowledged, whether because of the patrilineal bias of my culture or my simple ignorance resulting from his early departure from my life. In particular, I became more aware of the ambiguities and internal divisions in my own life, since they were so clear

---

4. For the history see Lavender, *Story of Cyprus Mines*.

in his, at least from my vantage point ninety years later. His deep piety was encased in a blinkered ethnocentrism. His self-discipline could be shattered by emotion-laden frustration as his perfectionism encountered the bedrock of human frailty and perversity. His professional exactitude was often unable to accommodate the rough edges of human failure or finitude, whether in his relations with colleagues, workers, or even family.

Among the materials unearthed by my sister was a plain black journal of his daily life at the mine. In it I discovered not only his constant struggles with workers, machinery, and materials, but also the tragic details of a mine fire that claimed several lives and precipitated a breakup with his senior colleague that resulted in his family's early departure from Cyprus. As a lasting mark of this experience, mine safety became a major part of his subsequent work at the US Bureau of Mines. None of this had ever reached my ears.

Above all, through my conversations and experiences on Cyprus, I saw the tension between the progress brought to Cyprus by the industrialization occasioned by the mine and the continued subordination of Cyprus to the economic and political forces of its wider world. My grandfather participated in the colonial empire of Great Britain, even though he was an American called to a task of engineering. I came to know more pointedly how deep is the division within us between our desires for all the technological devices made possible by mining and our concern for the earth's perilous state of pollution and ecological imbalance. It was a world and heritage both opposed to the ecological concerns of *Red Clay, Blood River*, but also a doorway into the real-world challenge of finding a more sustainable and harmonious relationship between human enterprise and earthly welfare. Both were currents running within my own life.

Not only did the Cyprus experience enlarge and complicate my self-understanding and my ecological awareness, it also deepened my understanding of the complexity of reconciliation. The mine lies beside the buffer zone that has divided Cyprus since 1974 into the Greek-speaking Republic of Cyprus to the south and the Turkish-speaking Republic of North Cyprus to the north. The forced removal of members of the two ethnic groups had left behind not only the mine's polluted tailings in the buffer zone, but a tangle of unrealized restitution for property that embitters people to this day. Just as this division prevented efforts to clean up the tailings from the mine operations of my grandfather's day, it also erected huge challenges for all those who continue to work on re-uniting the island in some sort of federal polity. My experiences on Cyprus will always affect how I think about reconciliation, federalism, and ecological integrity, not to mention my own life.

In particular, I was brought once again to the critical work of memory in the process of reconciliation. Cyprus has a long memory stretching back to Homer and beyond. One of the first things Constantinos Xydas, the mine's director, said to me was that the mine is mentioned in Book 11 of Homer's *Iliad*, where Agamemnon receives the bronze for his shield from the King of Cyprus. He saw himself as the current steward of that mine, seeking ways to bring its four-thousand-year history to an ecologically satisfying close, with access to the tailings in the buffer zone being one of his biggest challenges. He was already beginning the process of turning the mine area into a park with accommodations for large gatherings for concerts and similar events.

Through my little work of lifting up rare photographs and documents from my own family's past, including some artifacts, I hoped to make a small contribution to building up a common memory of the island through which its people could envision a new life of justice and unity. It has been one of those few moments we get in life where we can clearly see the relation between our little work and the big work around us. The little historical artifact I produced has not only contributed to the work of memory and hoped-for reconciliation on Cyprus, but also, as an artifact, it has been received as just one more proof of the outside's imperial control of the island's welfare. I learned once again that any effort at remembering history also becomes an object in contemporary struggles over its meaning. We ultimately control neither our own lives nor the works we leave behind. This realization drives me back to the importance of integrity in what we create in the present as well as a humility about our powers.

In a strange way the unexpected experience of recovering personal as well as collective memory on Cyprus brought together various strands of my thought in a profound manner. Not only was this a personal journey, it also exposed yet more facets of the ecological concerns with land that stretched back to my childhood. Moreover, it presented in a demanding form the struggle for a federal republic whose covenant would embrace the ecological integrity of the island itself. In the longing of its people to give voice to a rich plurality of life in their Cypriot-inflected Turkish, Greek, and English, it was a signal expression of the human drive toward the full covenantal publicity I had first described in *God's Federal Republic*.

In its division between Islam and Greek Orthodoxy (not to mention Armenian, Latin, and Russian traditions), Cyprus also brings to the fore the religious dimensions of the struggle that I studied in *Religion, Federalism, and the Struggle for Public Life*. The Greek flags flying at Orthodox churches and the Turkish flags at mosques to the north, reminded me of the deeply problematic American flags in the sanctuaries of churches across the United States. There can be no "secular" solution to Cyprus's federalist puzzle without dealing with these cultural and religious facts.

All of these images from my Cyprus experience have accompanied me as I helped plan the Interfaith Peace Conferences at Lake Junaluska. As Sylvia and I led the capstone conference on "The Arts of Peace: Imagining the Way," in 2019 we came to the end of the "thus far" of this reflection on how I have made my way through my life's complex terrain of ethics, worship, and woodcraft.

Recollection

IN TRYING TO GRASP the rich complexity of our lives we instinctively turn to vibrant metaphors. Those of craft, journey, and weaving have arisen constantly to guide my imagination in this effort of memory and articulation. I am at some deep level a maker, a craftsman, and my life can be understood as one of making connections, not only among events but among people, ideas, and wood. It has been shaped by very different milieus, and so this work of connection has taken place as a journey of constant new discovery, of turns into unexpected places that have challenged my thinking and action. And it has had some continuous strands of thought and conviction interwoven with many threads of new experience. In this respect we realize that the full tapestry of our lives is never completed, never fully seen. In this brief memoir I have identified numerous threads that have composed the weaving of my life. Through this metaphor I can also see some patterns that emerge to guide the eye of my recollection.

From my earliest years I have sought to weave together public life with personal spirituality. This work has taken many forms. It was present in my fascination with the way the body had been used as a metaphor to mobilize and shape our action in the public life of associations. It was present as I made my way through the struggle of my divorce and re-marriage, in which the demands of inner communion had to be connected to the publics created by our own and our ancestors' covenants. And it is present in the way I have sought to grasp the deep connections between the body of earth, our own bodies, and the public life through which we have to respond to the challenge of radical climate change.

The church, the ecclesia, has been for me the place of intersection between the deeply personal, mysterious, and transcendent realm of the spirit and the public world of connections, associations, constitutions, and covenants. In its symbolism, ritual, and prayerful poetics the deep yearnings of the Spirit are formed into legitimating convictions, practices, and dispositions for human life together on this earth. But the patriarchal and monarchical symbolism of its founding has lost its purchase and power in a world longing for democratic assembly and self-governance, and so I have struggled to articulate a new symbolism and ritual for its prayer, ritual, and song.

I found in concepts of covenant, public, and the oikos key ways to understand the dynamic connections between the life of the Spirit, the historic drama of our public worlds, and the evolving life of the earth. The complex concept of covenant as embracing people, land, and God also underlay the OIKOS Project and my effort to connect person, family, land, ecclesia, and public life. Even as I have re-articulated it, I have found a deep resonance with the conviction of my ancestors in faith and life that covenanting lies at the heart of what it is to be the ecclesia, the public life, of Christ on this special earth.

In the concept of covenantal publicity I tried to capture the drive toward full personal expression as well as a common world of mutuality. Behind it lies a classic republican commitment to conversation, persuasion, and negotiation in the face of patriarchal despotism and domination. This commitment to open public life has always been held within a framework of covenantal obligation, whether in the deep covenants of creation, the covenantal wisdom of the heirs of Biblical faith, or the constitutional covenants of particular republics. In the fullness of our covenantal bonds we experience a yearning for a greater realization—in St. Paul's words, a "groaning of creation" for its perfection.

This drive for full covenantal publicity in my life took a different form in the ethos and work of craftsmanship. In tangible objects of wood I sought to create a public environment for worship, specifically a worship grounded in circle conversations at the heart of genuine public life. At the same time, I tried to create an aesthetic work to elicit the natural beauty in wood as well as in the forms attuned to our deepest inner sensibilities. In many ways, I realize, this longing for craft perfection stands in deep tension with the fleeting world of public life, just as Hannah Arendt had pointed out in the distinction between work and action in *The Human Condition*. It is a tension that has run all through my life and will continue to the end.

Making My Way in Ethics, Worship, and Wood

The ethos of craft and joinery, with its concern to connect many diverse components into a useful whole, characterized much of my earlier work as I sought to make my way through the diverse worlds of theology and the social sciences. Under the impact of my own life experience it then yielded to a more narrative awareness in my later work, one open to the particularities of durable commitment as well as the exaltations of vibrant joy.

In this latter period, the intertwining of aesthetics and ethics, beauty and justice, has been realized not only in works of wood, but also in my efforts in poetry and song. Both of these efforts seek to connect the often inchoate impulses of my inner intuitions with the media of communication, mutuality, and covenanted worlds of meaning.

The tapestry fragments that emerge in this account are as much products of tension as of harmony. Some have emerged because of circumstance and event—my origins along the Potomac, my experience in marriage, parenthood, and divorce, the collapse of our family's farm, and the very different contexts for my teaching in America, Germany, India, and South Africa. Others emerge from the logic of earlier thoughts—the dynamic of covenantal publicity, the OIKOS Project, the round tables. In all of them I can now see the many dimensions of reconciliation as a kind of organizing pattern drawing them together into a more coherent whole. It is a work that is never fully realized, a way that is never completed. It exists in its hopes as much as in its accomplishments. But without that longing and that work our lives lose their sense of grounding in the eternal creativity supporting all of life. Our lives are an uncompleted song, but not without a straining for an encompassing reconciliation.

Bibliography

Adams, James Luther. *Voluntary Associations: Socio-cultural Analyses and Theological Interpretation.* Edited by J. Ronald Engel. Chicago: Exploration, 1986.

———. *The Prophethood of All Believers.* Edited by George K. Beach. Boston: Beacon, 1986.

Akenson, Donald Harman. *God's Peoples: Covenant and Land in South Africa, Israel, and Ulster.* Ithaca: Cornell University Press, 1992.

Arendt, Hannah. *The Human Condition.* Garden City NJ: Doubleday-Anchor, 1959.

———. *On Revolution.* New York: Viking, 1965.

Baum, Gregory, "Ecumenical Theology: A New Approach." *The Ecumenist* 19, no. 5 (July–August 1981) 65–78.

Bellah, Robert. "Civil Religion in America." *Daedalus* 96 (1967) 1–21.

———. *The Broken Covenant: American Civil Religion in Time of Trial.* New York: Seabury, 1975.

Bosselman, Klaus, and Engel, J. Ronald. *The Earth Charter: A Framework for Global Governance.* Amsterdam, The Netherlands: KIT Publishers, 2010.

Brown, Norman O. *Life Against Death: The Psychoanalytical Meaning of History.* New York: Vintage, 1959.

Cage, John. *Silence.* Middletown, CT: Wesleyan University Press, 1961.

Conradie, Ernst. *Hope for the Earth: Vistas on a New Century.* Eugene, OR: Wipf and Stock, 2005.

De Gruchy, John W. *Christianity and Democracy.* Cambridge: Cambridge University Press, 1995.

———. *Christianity, Art and Transformation: Theological Aesthetics in the Struggle for Justice.* Cambridge: Cambridge University Press, 2001.

Deutsch, Karl W. *The Nerves of Government: Models of Political Communication and Control.* New York: The Free Press, 1966.

Duchrow, Ulrich. *Christenheit und Weltverantwortung: Traditionsgeschichte und systematische Struktur der Zweireichelehre.* Stuttgart: Ernst Klett, 1970.

Elazar Daniel J. *The Covenant Tradition in Politics.* Vol. I, *Covenant and Polity in Biblical Israel: Biblical Foundations and Jewish Expressions.* New Brunswick, NJ: Transaction, 1994.

BIBLIOGRAPHY

———. *The Covenant Tradition in Politics*. Vol. II, *Covenant and Commonwealth: From Christian Separation through the Protestant Reformation*. New Brunswick, NJ: Transaction, 1995.

———. *The Covenant Tradition in Politics*. Vol. III, *Covenant and Constitutionalism: The Covenant Tradition in Politics*. New Brunswick, NJ: Transaction, 1998.

———. *The Covenant Tradition in Politics*. Vol. IV, *Covenant and Civil Society: The Constitutional Matrix of Modern Democracy*. New Brunswick, NJ: Transaction, 1997.

Everett, William W., III. "Baptists and Politics: A Study of the Search for Cultural Relevance in the American Baptist Convention." Honors College BA Thesis, Wesleyan University, 1962.

———. "Between Augustine and Hildebrand: A Critical Response to Human Sexuality." *Proceedings of the Thirty-third Annual Convention of the Catholic Theological Society of America, June 7–10, 1978*. 33 (1979) 77–83.

———. "Body Thinking in Ecclesiology and Cybernetics." PhD Diss., Harvard University, 1970.

———. "Cybernetics and the Symbolic Body Model." *Zygon: Journal of Religion and Science* 7, no. 2 (June 1972) 98–109.

———. "Ecclesiology and Political Authority: A Dialogue with Hannah Arendt." *Encounter* (Indianapolis) 36, no. 1 (Winter 1975) 26–36.

———. "Land Ethics: Toward a Covenantal Model." In *American Society of Christian Ethics, 1979: Selected Papers from the Twentieth Annual Meeting*, 45–74. Waterloo, Ontario: Council on the Study of Religion, 1979.

———. "Liturgy and American Society: An Invocation to Ethical Analysis." *Anglican Theological Review* 56, no. 1 (January 1974) 16–34.

———. "Stewardship Through Trust and Cooperation." In *Stewardship Papers*. Spirituality Series, No. 3. 1–4. Chicago: Pax Christi USA, 1980.

———. "Vocation and Location: An Exploration in the Ethics of Ethics." *Journal of Religious Ethics* 5, no. 1 (Spring 1977) 91–112.

Everett, William Johnson. *Blessed Be the Bond: Christian Perspectives on Marriage and Family*. Minneapolis: Fortress Press, 1985. Reprinted 1990 by University Press of America. Third ed., rev., published by author through KDP, 2019.

———. "Communion Carpentry: A Conversation of Wood and Word." *The Christian Century*, 118, no. 2 (January 17, 2001) 6–7.

———. "Constitutional Order in United Methodism and American Culture." With Thomas E. Frank. In *Connectionalism: Ecclesiology, Mission, and Identity*, edited by Russell E. Richey and Dennis Campbell, 41–73. Nashville: Abingdon, 1997.

———. "Couples at Work: A Study in Patterns of Work, Family and Faith." With Sylvia Johnson Everett. In *Work, Family, and Religion in Contemporary Society*, edited by Nancy Tatom Ammerman and Wade Clark Roof, 305–29. New York: Routledge, 1995.

———. "Finding the Ethics in Architecture." *Faith and Form. Journal of the Interfaith Forum on Religion, Art, and Architecture* 33, no. 2 (2000) 21–23.

———. "Gathering at the Roundtable." In *Conflict and Communion: Reconciliation and Restorative Justice at Christ's Table*, edited by Thomas Porter, 121–29. Nashville, TN: Discipleship Resources, 2006.

———. *God's Federal Republic: Reconstructing Our Governing Symbol*. Mahwah, NJ: Paulist Press, 1988. Reprint Eugene, OR: Wipf & Stock, 2019.

Bibliography

———. *Gottes Bund und menschliche Öffentlichkeit. Ökumenische Existenz heute* 8. Translated by Gerd Decke. Munich: Christian Kaiser, 1991.

———. "Human Rights in the Church." In *Religious Human Rights in Global Perspective: Religious Perspectives*, edited by John Witte Jr., and Johann van der Vyver, 121–42. Dordrecht: Martinus Nijhoff, 1995.

———. "Journey Images and the Search for Reconciliation." *Journal of the Society of Christian Ethics* 23, no. 2 (Fall/Winter 2003) 155–78.

———. *Mining Memories in Cyprus 1923–25: Photographs, Correspondence, Reflections.* Published by William Johnson Everett as Kindle e-Book, 2017.

———. *Neue Öffentlichkeit in neuem Bund. Theologische Reflexionen zur Kirche in der Wende.* Heidelberg, Germany: Forschungsstätte der evangelischen Studiengemeinschaft, 1992.

———. "OIKOS: Convergence in Business Ethics." *Journal of Business Ethics* 5 (1985) 313–25.

———. *The Politics of Worship: Reforming the Language and Symbols of Liturgy.* Cleveland: United Church Press, 1999.

———. *Praying for God's Republic: A Proposal for Transforming our Worship.* Revised edition of *The Politics of Worship.* 2010. Available at http://williameverett.com/books-and-articles-free/.

———. "Public Works: Bridging the Gap Between Theology and Public Ethics." In *Theological Literacy for the Twenty-First Century*, edited by Rodney L. Petersen, 150–65. Grand Rapids: Eerdmans, 2002.

———. *Red Clay, Blood River.* William Johnson Everett through Booklocker, 2008.

———. *Religion, Federalism, and the Struggle for Public Life: Cases from Germany, India, and America.* New York: Oxford University Press, 1997.

———. "Ritual Wisdom and Restorative Justice." *Hamline Journal of Public Law and Policy* 25, no. 2 (Spring 2004) 347–54.

———. *Roundtable Worship: A Reflective Guide.* William Johnson Everett, 2010. Available at http://williameverett.com/books-and-articles-free/.

———. "Seals and Springboks: Theological Reflections on Constitutionalism and South African Culture." *Journal of Theology for Southern Africa* 101 (July 1998) 71–82.

———. "Serving the Church and Facing the Law: Virtues for Committee Members Evaluating a Pastor." In *Practice What You Preach: Virtues, Ethics, and Power in the Lives of Pastoral Ministers and Their Congregations*, edited by James F. Keenan and Joseph Kotva Jr., 268–79. Franklin, WI: Sheed and Ward, 1999.

———. "Shared Parenthood in Divorce: The Parental Covenant and Custody Law." *Journal of Law and Religion* 2, no. 1 (1984) 85–99.

———. "Sunday Monarchists and Monday Citizens?" *The Christian Century* 106, no. 16 (May 10, 1989) 503–5.

———. "Transformation at Work." In *Religious Education as Social Transformation*, edited by Allen Moore, 153–76. Birmingham: Religious Education Press, 1989.

———. *Turnings: Poems of Transformation.* Eugene, OR: Resource Publications, 2013.

———. "Versöhnung zwischen Heimkehr und Zukunft: Eine Fallstudie aus dem amerikanischen Vietnam-Krieg." In *Politik der Versöhnung*, hrsg. Gerhard Beestermöller und Hans-Richard Reuter, 169–80. Stuttgart: W. Kohlhammer, 2002.

———. "With the Grain: Woodworking, Spirituality, and the Struggle for Justice." *Journal of Theology for Southern Africa* 123 (November 2005) 6–15.

Bibliography

Everett, William Johnson, and T.J. Bachmeyer. *Disciplines in Transformation: A Guide to Theology and the Behavioral Sciences.* With T. J. Bachmeyer. Washington: University Press of America, 1979. Rev. ed. published by William Johnson Everett through KDP, 2019.

Everett, William Johnson, and John W. de Gruchy. *Sawdust and Soul: A Conversation about Woodworking and Spirituality.* Eugene, OR: Cascade, 2015.

Fowler, James W. *Stages of Faith: The Psychology of Human Development and the Quest for Meaning.* New York: Harper-Collins, 1981.

Freud, Sigmund. *Civilization and Its Discontents.* Translated by James Strachey. New York: W. W. Norton, 1961.

Fustel de Coulanges, Numa Denis. *The Ancient City: A Study on the Religion, Laws, and Institutions of Greece and Rome.* Garden City, NJ: Doubleday, 1955 [1864].

Gore, Al. *The Assault on Reason: Our Information Ecosystem, from the Age of Print to the Age of Trump.* New York: Penguin, 2017.

Gustafson, James M. *Treasure in Earthen Vessels: The Church as Human Community.* New York: Harper & Row, 1961.

———. *A Sense of the Divine: The Natural Environment from a Theocentric Perspective.* Cleveland: Pilgrim Press, 1994.

Gutierrez, Gustavo. *A Theology of Liberation.* Maryknoll, NY: Orbis, 1973.

Habermas, Jürgen. "The Public Sphere." *New German Critique* 3 (Fall 1974) 360–75.

———. *Legitimation Crisis.* Translated by Thomas McCarthy. Boston: Beacon Press, 1975.

Hartshorne, Charles. *The Divine Relativity: A Social Conception of God.* 2d ed. New Haven: Yale University Press, 1964.

Holl, Karl. "Die Geschichte des Worts Beruf." *Gesammelte Aufsätze zur Kirchengeschichte.* Bd. III. 189–219. Darmstadt: Wissenschaftliche Buchgesellschaft, 1965.

Huber, Wolfgang. *Gerechtigkeit und Recht: Grundlinien christlicher Rechtsethik.* Gütersloh: Christian Kaiser, 1996.

———. *Kirche und Öffentlichkeit.* Stuttgart: Ernst Klett, 1973.

Lavender, David. *The Story of Cyprus Mines Corporation.* San Marino, CA: Huntington Library, 1962.

Levinson, Daniel J. *The Seasons of a Man's Life.* New York: Ballentine, 1991.

Lutheran World Federation Department of Studies. *The Identity of the Church and Its Service to the Whole Human Being: Summary, Analysis, Interpretation.* 2 vols. Geneva: Lutheran World Federation Department of Studies, 1977.

Macpherson, C. B. *The Political Theory of Possessive Individualism.* New York: Oxford University Press, 1965.

Mannheim, Karl. *Ideology and Utopia: An Introduction to the Sociology of Knowledge.* Translated by Louis Wirth and Edward Shils. New York: Harcourt, 1936.

Mathews, Shailer. *The Atonement and the Social Process.* New York: Macmillan, 1930.

Miller, Francis Trevelyan, Editor in chief. *The Photographic History of the Civil War: In Ten Volumes.* New York: The Review of Reviews, 1911.

Moltmann, Jürgen. *The Crucified God: The Crucified Christ as the Foundation and Criticism of Christian Theology.* Minneapolis: Fortress, 1993. Original German edition 1974.

Myers, Henry. *Medieval Kingship.* Chicago: Nelson-Hall, 1982.

Niebuhr, H. Richard. *Christ and Culture.* New York: Harper & Row, 1951.

———. *The Responsible Self: An Essay on Christian Moral Philosophy.* New York: Harper & Row, 1963.

Bibliography

———. *Radical Monotheism and Western Culture: With Supplementary Essays.* New York: Harper, 1960.

———. *The Social Sources of Denominationalism.* New York: Henry Holt, 1929.

Parsons, Talcott. *The Social System.* New York: The Free Press, 1965.

———. "Christianity and Modern Industrial Society." In *Sociological Theory, Values, and Sociocultural Change. Essays in Honor of Pitirim A. Sorokin,* edited by Edward A. Tiryakian, 33–70. New York: The Free Press, 1963.

Porter, Thomas, ed. *Conflict and Communion: Reconciliation and Restorative Justice at Christ's Table.* Nashville, TN: Discipleship Resources, 2006.

Sahi, Jyoti. *Holy Ground: A New Approach to the Mission of the Church in India.* Auckland: Pace, 1998.

———. *Stepping Stones: Reflections on the Theology of Indian Christian Culture.* Bangalore: Asian Trading Corporation, 1986.

Stackhouse, Max L. *Ethics and the Urban Ethos.* Boston: Beacon, 1972.

Stassen, Glen H. *Just Peacemaking: Transforming Initiatives for Justice and Peace.* Louisville, KY: Westminster/John Knox, 1992.

Teilhard de Chardin, Pierre. *The Phenomenon of Man.* Translated by Bernard Wall. New York: Harper and Row, 1961.

Thangaraj, M. Thomas. *The Crucified Guru: An Experiment in Cross-Cultural Christology* Nashville, TN: Abingdon, 1994.

Troeltsch, Ernst. *The Social Teaching of the Christian Churches.* Translated by Olive Wyon. New York: Harper and Row, 1960.

Underwood, Kenneth W. *Protestant and Catholic: Religious and Social Interaction in an Industrial Community.* Boston: Beacon Press, 1957.

Walzer, Michael. *The Revolution of the Saints: A Study in the Origins of Radical Politics* Cambridge, MA: Harvard University Press, 1968.

Weber, Max. *The Protestant Ethic and the Spirit of Capitalism.* Translated by Talcott Parsons. New York: Charles Scribner's Sons, 1958.

———. *From Max Weber: Essays in Sociology.* Edited and translated by H. H. Gerth and C. Wright Mills. New York: Oxford University Press, 1958.

Whitehead, Alfred North. *Adventures of Ideas.* New York: Macmillan Company, 1933.

———. *Religion in the Making.* New York: Macmillan, 1926.

———. *Science and the Modern World.* New York: Macmillan, 1925.

Williams, Roger. *A Key into the Language of America* [1643]. 5th ed. Providence: Rhode Island and Providence Plantations, Inc., 1936. Reprint Bedford, MA: Applewood Books, [1997].

Wren, Brian. *What Language Shall I Borrow? God-Talk in Worship: A Male Response to Feminist Theology.* New York: Crossroad, 1989.

www.ingramcontent.com/pod-product-compliance
Lightning Source LLC
Chambersburg PA
CBHW050827160426
43192CB00010B/1921